A Volume in
Ideas in Critical Postmodernism

Volume One

Work and Organization: The Aesthetic Dimension

Ideas in Critical Postmodernism
Series Editor: David Boje

Volume 1: **Work and Organization: The Aesthetic Dimension**
Adrian Carr and Philip Hancock (eds.)
ISBN 978-0-9817032-5-1.

Volume 2: **Discourses & Paradigms**
Susanne M. Fest & Darin A. Arsenault (eds.)
Forthcoming 2009.

Volume 3: **Management & Goodness**
Heather Hopfl & Ron Beadle (eds.)
Forthcoming 2009.

Volume 4: **Narrative & Time**
Eric Kramer (eds.)
Forthcoming 2009.

Ideas in Critical Postmodernism:
Volume One

Work and Organization: The Aesthetic Dimension

Edited by
Adrian Carr & Philip Hancock

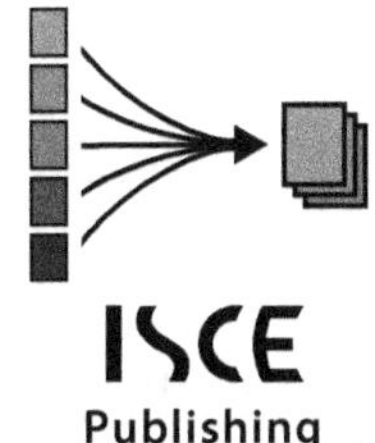

3810 N 188th Ave
Litchfield Park, AZ 85340

Cover Image: Technospirit by Virginia Maria Romero.

About the artist: Virginia Maria Romero (agzromero@zianet.com) is an award winning artist whose works reflect original contemporary designs that express the distinctive voice of their creator. The style, color and compositions of her acrylics as well as her retablos continue to exhibit her uniqueness and creative quality. To see more of her art, http://www.artederomero.com/.

Work and Organization: The Aesthetic Dimension
Ideas in Critical Postmodernism: Volume 1
Edited by: Adrian Carr and Philip Hancock

Library of Congress Control Number: 2009922907

ISBN13: 978-0-9817032-5-1

Printed in the United States of America.

CONTENTS

Series Editor's Introduction to *Ideas in Critical Postmodernism* Volume 1

I am proud and excited to introduce the new series: *Ideas in Critical Postmodernism.* We are exhibiting the best *Tamara: Journal of Critical Organization Inquiry* has to offer.

The cover for our first volume is by world class artist, Virginia Maria Romero, a painting she calls, 'Technospirit.' To see more of her art visit ,http://www.artederomero.com. Vriginia Maria and I have joined art and business forces to engage local arts organizations in a critical investigation of our local arts economy, and its aesthetics.

The first volume of the book series is *Work, Aesthetics and Organization* edited by Adrian Carr and Philip Hancock. To continue my storytelling, New Mexico has rather poor arts economies in the southern part of the state, and the the more renowned Santa Fe and Taos to the north. Local work and aesthetics and arts organizations exhibit a contestation, a competition to advance and affirm their arts scenes.

The second volume of this book series will be *Discourse and Paradigms* edited by Susanne M. Fest and Darin A. Arsenault. I like storytelling, so here is another verse. There are so many artistic paradigms moving into New Mexico, into Dona Ana County where I live, that a multiplicity of discourses flourish. We have tried various open space and world cafe methods of discourse, but somehow its not the kind of dialogic imagination that inspired Bakhtin. Instead there is a lot of monologue calling itself dialogue, and efforts to enforce or impose consensus hegemony by the powers that be. Nothing dialogical in the herd of discourses, that remain disembodied, disestablished, just so many lines on a flip chart, with most of the good stuff invisible to the process of recording.

The third volume in the book series will be *Management and Goodness* edited by Heather Hopfl and Rod Beadie. To continue my rant. There is an ethics of goodness that those who manage the arts and culture of our county, be they in the public, private or grassroots establishment, can not seem to sort out. An ethics of goodness is something we would like to meet. It sounds like its Aristotelean, but more to the point its a kind of Bakhtinian answerability (or I would like it to be so). There are these once occurent times in the moment of being where people managing and being managed could chose to act, to intervene in the now, and bring some different 'being' artist about.

The fourth planned volume in the book series is *Narrative and Time* edited by Eric Kramer. Now you now what I will say. That narrative is so established, so retrospective, so whole, so caught up in beginning, middle, and end that it can not recognize other forms of storytelling. To me, those other forms are living story, the nowness of being in the moment, and my telling is in the middle, no ending, no beginning, but I have to tell you this other living story that relates to others' being. And second, there is this 'antenarrative,' bet on the future, a prospective sensemaking, a morph, a changeling that is ever part of emergence, moving disorder into order, finding solace in chaos to bring about something that never was in narrative, something falling out of living story webs.

So there you have it a storytelling introduction to a book series, *Ideas in Critical Postmodernism.* Perhaps I am the last postmodernist still breathing, still using the burned out word. I don't mean every kind of postmodernism, I mean one wed to Critical Theory (capitalized, to represent old school, Frankfurt style, and before that Nietzsche). *Tamara Journal* once had postmodern its its title, but no one reads postmodernism anymore. So we dropped it and I am thankful to Kurt Richardson and ISCE Publishing for rescuing it from the dust bowl of history.

David M. Boje
11 February, 2009
New Mexico

Editorial

Art and Aesthetics at Work: An Overview

Adrian Carr & Philip Hancock

Introduction

Over recent years the field of organization studies has exhibited an increasing interest in the aesthetic dimension of work and its organization. Whilst this interest may have been awakened, more generally, by the publication of such philosophically oriented works as Eagleton's (1990) *The ideology of the aesthetic* and Welsch's (1997) *Undoing aesthetics*, it must also be understood in relation to a series of developments within the field itself over the last three decades or so. The shift from an almost exclusively objectivist approach to the analysis of organizational practice exemplified in Weick's (1969) *The social psychology of organizing* and Silverman's (1970) *The theory of organizations*, for example, signified a significant step along the path towards an acceptance of the relevance of sensuality to understanding the rich tapestry that is organizational life. Of equal, and perhaps greater contemporary importance, has been the groundbreaking work focusing on manifestations of organizational culture and symbolism (Alvesson & Berg, 1992; Turner, 1990) with the *Third international conference on organizational symbolism* (1987) whose theme was 'The symbolics of corporate artifacts', particularly noteworthy, resulting as it did in the publication of a selection of papers (see Gagliardi, 1990) that helped to inform and focus the field of organization studies on the presence of an aesthetic sensibility.

Subsequently, a range of published contributions to the field have been forthcoming, including individual journal articles (Carr, 1997; Carr & Zanetti, 2000; Guillén, 1997; Rustead, 1999) thematic editions of journals (*Or-*

ganization, 1996), chapters in edited collections (Hancock & Tyler, 2000; Thompson, Warhurst & Callaghan 2000), edited books (Linstead & Höpfl., 2000) and monographs (Strati, 1999), many of which have been characterized by the work and ideas of scholars who draw significantly on a range of radical traditions within the social sciences, including critical theory, post-structuralism and postmodernism. Furthermore, in addition to such academic and critically oriented offerings, more populist management writers are also starting to contribute significantly to the diffusion of aesthetic concepts throughout the business world. For example, building on the work of writers on corporate identity and design such as Olins (1989), the likes of Dickinson and Svensen (2000) have sought in their millennium manifesto, *Beautiful corporations: Corporate style in action*, to argue the case for an organizational aesthetic that expresses beauty and style through everything from physical design to corporate ethics and environmental responsibility.

It is to this embryonic, if albeit increasingly flourishing body of research and literature within management and business studies, which this volume seeks to both, contribute to, and help take beyond its current stage of development.

Rationale

Art and aesthetics at work, while an ambiguous title for a single volume is not one that was deliberately contrived to be so. Initially, it was conceived of simply as a description of the subject matter of the volume. That is, what the various contributors consider to be the role and opportunities that art and aesthetics are increasingly coming to play in the study and practice of work organizations. However, it quickly became clear that an alternative meaning, implicit within the title's semantic construction, also had great relevance for this volume. For, what many of the chapters contained within this collection are at pains to consider is not only the presence of art and aesthetics within the everyday life of the workplace, but equally, how these are increasingly put to work in the service of a range of organizational aspirations and goals or, alternatively, how they can provide a range of novel and informative insights into the structuring and maintenance of organizational activities, particularly those which rely upon the continued existence of asymmetrical relations of power and control. Aesthetic experience is thus differentially conceptualized at various stages throughout this volume, not only as an outcome of divergent terms of reference or theoretical agendas, but also as a consequence of the positioning and functioning that is ascribed to it within the organizational domain of work.

The existence of ambiguity should not, of course, provide any great surprise for those familiar with the equally ambiguous history of the aesthetic itself. While the origins of the concept can be traced back to antiquity, its contemporary usage remains highly contested. Originally conceived of in the work of Baumgarten (1753/1954), as the systematic study of sensual and affective dimension of human experience the everyday meaning and usage of the term has shifted and changed considerably over the subsequent centuries. Yet today, while it is still more likely to be understood in relation to the categorization and judgment of art, much of Baumgraten's original conception of its nature remains in evidence, particularly in work inspired by the critical interrogation of modernity associated with critical theory and postmodernism. Such a broad engagement with the aesthetic, as the realm of sensual experience, is also, therefore, as important to the work contained within this collection, as is its more traditional association with the realm of art and artistic practice.

Such divergences, ambiguities and contestations are therefore the lifeblood of the aesthetic and, as such it is our hope as the editors that through the mix of international and established writers and scholars, and new or emerging academics within the field of organization and management studies, we have been able to provide a taste of this. Furthermore, we also anticipate that in doing so we have produced a volume that may yet provide an insightful, eclectic, and perhaps in some cases iconoclastic, overview of the increasing relevance of aesthetics and aesthetic theory for the ongoing development of a critical understanding of contemporary work organizations.

About the Chapters in this Volume

The chapters in this volume owe their origins to a conference held at the University of Manchester in July 2001. This conference, *The second international critical management studies conference,* contained a stream on art and aesthetics which was convened by the editors of this volume. We would like to publicly thank Hugh Willmott and Irena Grugulis for allowing us to use this venue for what turned out to be one of the most well attended streams of the conference and a stream that yielded far too many excellent submissions for presentation. One of the aims of convening the stream was to subsequently put together a group of outstanding papers for a special issue of a journal and to possibly form the nucleus for a major edited work on the same topic. David Boje was extremely supportive of this project and agreed to the development of a special issue of the journal, *TAMARA*, on the topic of art and aesthetics.

The chapters that constitute this volume should be understood as being inter-related, and are clearly focussed upon the topic of art and aesthetics. Notwithstanding, the chapters in this volume can be seen to speak to three major themes which could be broadly described as: Art and aesthetics *as a way of knowing organization*; the organization of *work itself is an aesthetically ordered activity*; and, *critical engagements with aesthetics at work.*

In the next chapter, *Art as a form of knowledge: The implications for critical management*, Adrian Carr emphasizes how art and aesthetics represents a way of knowing organization. Carr brings a critical theory perspective to the proposition that art is a form of knowledge and as having a language-like character that incites philosophical reflection. The critical theorists that Carr relies upon to build his case are Theodor Adorno, Walter Benjamin and Herbert Marcuse—all scholars associated with the Institut für Sozialforschung (the Institute for Social Research) which, because of its initial establishment in Frankfurt University, is commonly referred to as 'the Frankfurt School'. It might be recalled that the scholars associated with the Frankfurt School rejected the logico-rational tradition in which it was presumed that in the social sciences, like the natural sciences, there was an absolute truth capable of discovery through the scientific method. For these scholars, what passes for truth and knowledge in the social sciences could not be detached from the knowing subjects—knowledge always has to be conceived as mediated through society and has a dialectic 'nature' in the interplay of the particular and the universal, of the moment and totality (see Carr, 2000). It was in this context that the aforementioned scholars of the Frankfurt School conceived art and aesthetics as not some separate order as such, but instead as having a co-determined link to the 'otherness' it putatively sought to escape. The key issue here, for some of these scholars, is that on the one hand, art is mimetic and induces mimetic behavior in the viewer. Art mimics or carries resemblance. On the other hand, there is an enigmatic face to a work of art in as much as it carries discrepancy between projected images and their actuality. It is in this very act of an expression of non-identity with itself that art was considered to induce critical reflection.

The chapter explores the work of the surrealists to highlight the manner in which this critical reflection is induced. The intention of the surrealists was to break the rational 'language' of correspondence to induce new associations with the objects and images and to transcend the control, presence and even the overt intention of the 'author' of the work. Many of the works of the surrealists, for example, involved producing discomfort or 'shock' (an "estrangement-effect") through the juxtaposition of objects being placed in unfamiliar settings. The production of an estrangement-effect is discussed in terms of the dialectic dynamic that was championed by some of the Frankfurt School scholars. The chapter concludes with a discussion of how this work of the Frankfurt School scholars and the exploration of art and aesthetics, in particular, may provide a valuable optic through which the fields of management and organization studies might be reflexively explored—to perhaps 'see' anew issues for which we have, at best, had a superficial understanding.

This theme of art and aesthetics as being a way of knowing is also conspicuous in the next chapter which is by Watkins and King. In their chapter, entitled *Organizational performance: A view from the arts*, they tackle the issue of organizational performance, and the utility a more artistic sensibility could have for its evaluation and pursuit. Noting how the mainstream literature concerned with enhancing performance in organizations tends to follow strategies associated with the rule driven scienticism of early 20th management thought, they consider how this has generated the illusion that it is through the establishment of regulatory frameworks that the complex and unpredictable reality of organizational life can be geared towards optimizing performance.

In response to what the authors consider to be the inadequacies of this tradition, they provide an engaging re-evaluation of a series of historical breaks within the art world that were themselves brought about by the need to challenge a rule-grounded orthodoxy similar to that alluded to above. Richly illustrating their argument with the work of Cézanne, Picasso, James and Kafka, amongst others, the authors suggest that it was only with the break form the rules of perspectivism and realism that art finally became able to represent reality in all its richness and variation. As a consequence of this observation, they propose that management should perhaps also learn to incorporate a mode of thinking that would facilitate a movement outside of the traditional rule bound structures of organizational evaluation. One that may assist management to grasp the totality of organizational life in all its diversity and heterogeneity and, in doing so, provide a far more responsive guide to requisite organizational action in the search for appropriate levels of performativity.

The second of the themes or major currents within this volume—the idea that the organization of work itself is an aesthetically ordered activity—can be noted in the next two chapters in this volume. Nick Nissley, Steven S. Taylor and Orville Butler, take us into the sphere of organizational song and a consideration of its structuring effects on the action on both organizational employees and consumers. Reminding us that while the study of organization discourse has been extended to a range of areas, until now that of song—and particularly its lyrical content—has been largely overlooked. However, in their chapter, entitled *The power of organizational song: An organizational discourse and aesthetic expression of organizational culture,* they demonstrate how song can provide significant insights into the relations of meaning that circulate within the workplace.

Focusing particularly on the corporate songs of a major US home appliance manufacturer, the authors present us with what they term an archeological approach to the study of organizational life. That is, they set out to uncover and consider particular fragments of an organization's activities, in this instance its songs, as a means of gaining insight into the culture of the whole. Illustrating extensively their descriptive passages with extracts from a range of songs, they go onto develop a theoretically informed analysis of the ways in which such songs can be understood both to reflect the actuality of the existing organizational culture while, at the same time, function as a technology of organizational power that both enables and constrains its membership and those who came into contact with it. As such, songs can perhaps best be understood as technologies of mediation, operating at the interface between the subjective and objective dimensions of organizational experience.

The idea that the organization of work itself is an aesthetically ordered activity can also be noted in the chapter by Nancy Harding. Harding explores the relationship between aesthetics and the ordering of the human body. This author builds on previous work concerned with what has been referred to as *aesthetic labour* (Hancock & Tyler, 2000; Warhurst & Nickson, in press). Harding takes a particular and unique look at the bodies of organizational managers, and the role aesthetic labour plays in the structuring of their own subordination to the imperatives of capitalist organization. This highly engaging chapter provides an extensive theoretical framework for its subsequent analysis drawing, in particular, on a Foucauldian tradition of critique directed at uncovering the simultaneous process of subjectification/objectification the managerial body experiences as it goes about its everyday organizational activities.

This chapter brings to the foreground the proposition that it is not only the employee's bodies that are sculpted and worked on so as to generate an organizationally appropriate embodied aesthetic, but also managers, who are both subjectified in that they are self-constituted as a symbol of "conformity, rigidity and obedience", while at the same time embodying an objectified organizational aesthetic that is amenable to the gaze of the Other. The embodied process of management is thus itself an aesthetically ordered activity, one that functions both as a symbol of organizational power and a technology of internalized control, acting back onto the manager who is trapped within his/her own corporeal 'iron cage'.

In the final two chapters in this volume, we encounter the authors addressing a similar theme in as much as they both seek to self-consciously critically engage with aesthetics at work. In a chapter concerned with the question of organizational architecture, Karen Dale and Gibson Burrell address critically the relationship between corporate architecture, alienation and identity. Grounded in the emerging field of critical management studies, and its somewhat eclectic mix of influences, they bring both Benjamin's notion of the *dazzle* and Welsch's particular conceptualization of the process of *anaestheticization* into play as they probe the organizational sensorium, and its relationship to the built environment of experience. Beginning with an interrogation of the polysemetic character of the aesthetic, and drawing out from this the concept of anesthetization, the authors lead us on a journey from the imagery of Huxley's *Brave new world,* via Benjamin's Parisian experience of *phantasmagoria*, to the *dazzling* realm of modernist organizational architecture. Here, they stop to reflect upon the politics of such architecture, noting the political emasculation that the modernist style underwent during its cultural transplantation from the cultural context of European avant-gardism to the rational requirements of American cultural and material mass production.

Nevertheless, in doing so, they expose the functioning of an alternative political agenda, one driven by the urge to simultaneously dazzle, and anesthetize its spatial captives. This can be achieved by the over-stimulation of one sense (most likely the ocular sense) at the cost of the de-sensitization of the accompanying senses, thus limiting the range of the individual human sensorium. However, it is also noted how it is not only those who encounter such organizations that potentially undergo such a desensitization or anestheticization process. Those who labour in, and build and design such places are drawn into relations of economic and political subservience that also anesthetizes their relationship with the world they, in large part, create. Management, the authors note therefore, is not simply concerned with the management of minds and hearts, but equally, the management of the senses—and it is this realization that critical management studies must arrive at if it is to pursue reflexively its challenge to the alienating consequences of contemporary organizational activity.

The final chapter is entitled *Aestheticizing the world of organization—creating beautiful untrue things* and is written by Philip Hancock. While representing a departure from the theme of architecture found in the previous chapter, it continues the critical tenor reflecting on what the author considers to be the negative implications of the emergence of a highly managerialist genre of texts concerned with the appropriation and management of organizational aesthetics; or as the title of this collection suggests, the act of putting 'aesthetics to work'.

Driven empirically by a critical analysis of several examples of such texts, and theoretically informed by the work of Theodor Adorno, Wolfgang Welsch and Sjtepan Mestrovic, amongst others, at the heart of this chapter is a spirited defence of what the author considers to be the unique role aesthetic experience and judgment is capable of contributing to the process of human emancipation, and the threat this faces from the subsequent imposition of an organizational logic. Referring to the possible emergence of a condition of post-aestheticism such a concern revolves around a theme similar to that discussed by Dale and Burrell, namely that by adorning the world in corporate imagery, and thus reducing aesthetic experience to "little more than just another repository of mechanically produced, instrumentally oriented codes and symbols", threatens both a process of cultural anesthetization, as well as a neutralization of the critical, and thus emancipatory, potential of aesthetic experience.

The chapter concludes with a clear assertion of distrust of those who champion the incorporation of aesthetic values and practices into the organizational realm. Locating the potential struggle between the non-conceptual nature of aesthetic experience and the rigidly conceptual, and inevitably instrumental, character of managerial planning and activity within the broader struggle between modernist rationality and the sensual, corporeal dynamic of Being, Hancock bemoans such developments as yet a further example of the disenchantment of the modern world. A world that while increasingly spectacular, adorned as it is in its corporate livery, is simultaneously rendered sterile, as aesthetic experience is reduced to a value identical to that generated through the reception of the standardized and rationalized aesthetics of corporate organization.

References

Alvesson, M. and Berg, P. (1992). *Corporate culture and organizational symbolism.* Berlin: de Gruyter.

Baumgarten, A. (1954). *Reflections on poetry* (K. Aschenbrenner & W. Holter, Eds. and Trans.). Berkeley, CA: University of California. (Original work published 1735)

Carr, A. (1997). Burrell at play: Countering linearity by entering the land of the 'dragons'. *Administrative Theory and Praxis, 19,* 408-413.

Carr, A. (2000). Critical theory and the management of change in organizations. In Special Issue on Critical Theory (A. Carr, Ed.). *Journal of Organizational Change Management, 13,* 208-220.

Carr, A. and Zanetti, L. (2000). The emergence of a surrealist movement and its vital 'estrangement-effect' in organisation studies. *Human Relations, 52,* 891-921.

Dickinson, P. and Svensen, N. (2000). *Beautiful corporations: Corporate style in action.* London: Prentice Hall.

Eagleton, T. (1990). *The ideology of the aesthetic.* Oxford: Blackwell.

Gagliardi, P. (Ed.). (1990). *Symbols and artifacts: Views of the corporate landscape.* New York: de Gruyter.

Guillén, M. (1997). Scientific management's lost aesthetic: Architecture, organization and the Taylorised beauty of the mechanical. *Administrative Science Quarterly, 42,* 682-715.

Hancock, P. and Tyler, M. (2000). "The look of love": Gender and the organization of aesthetics. In J. Hassard, R. Holliday & H. Willmott (Eds.), *Body and organization* (pp. 108-129). London: Sage.

Linstead, S. and Höpfl, H. (Ed.) (2000). *The aesthetics of organization.* London: Sage.

Olins, W. (1989). *Corporate identity: Making business strategy visible through design.* London: Thames and Hudson.

Organization, (1996). Special section on Aesthetics and organization, 3, 189-248.

Rustead, B. (1999). Socializing aesthetics and 'selling like gangbusters'. *Organization Studies, 20,* 641-658.

Silverman, D. (1970). *The theory of organizations: A sociological framework.* London: Heinemann.

Strati, A. (1999). *Organization and aesthetics.* London: Sage.

Thompson, P., Warhurst, C. and Callaghan, G. (2000). Human capital or capitalizing on humanity? Knowledge skills and competencies in interactive service work. In C. Prichard, R. Hull, M. Chumer & H. Willmott (Eds.), *Managing knowledge: Critical investigations of work and learning* (pp. 122-140). Basingstoke: Macmillan.

Turner, B. (Ed.) (1990). *Organizational symbolism.* Berlin: de Gruyter.

Warhurst, C. and Nickson, D. (in press). Rethinking aesthetics, organization and labour. *Organization.*

Welsch, W. (1997). *Undoing aesthetics.* London: Sage.

Weick, K. (1969). *The social psychology of organizing.* Reading, MA: Addison-Wesley.

Chapter 1
Art as a Form of Knowledge: The Implications for Critical Management

Adrian Carr

Introduction and Overview

Theodor Adorno (1970/1997) declared that art was a form of knowledge. In a somewhat related vein, his critical theorist colleague Herbert Marcuse (1956/1998) characterized art as a mode of cognition that is an alternative to positivism. The work of these two scholars is linked with the school of thought called "The Frankfurt School". Famous for its notion and development of "critical theory", the Frankfurt School's work was carried out initially at the Institut für Sozialforschung (the Institute for Social Research). This Institute was established in, but financially independent of, Frankfurt University. Founded in February 1923, a number of the scholars associated with the Institute found themselves drawn to *art and the aesthetics as arenas in which alternative ways of thinking and 'seeing' were possible.* For this group of scholars, in many ways, authentic art represented a "Great Refusal" (Marcuse, 1956/1998: 149) against totalizing forms of logic.

Drawing upon the work of the Frankfurt School, and specifically that of Adorno, Marcuse, and Walter Benjamin, this paper initially explores the mimetic and enigmatic qualities of art. Benjamin (1933/1999c) insisted that we all have a "mimetic faculty" (mimicry) responsible for producing and perceiving resemblance. For Benjamin, imitation is one of our most irresistible impulses. Benjamin, and Adorno, came to think of mimesis as an assimilation of self to other—a type of enactment behavior.

Adorno suggests that all autonomously generated artworks are enigmas in as much as they have a capacity to sustain a discrepancy between projected images and their actuality. They carry similarity while at the same time carrying difference. As will be noted later, Adorno (1970/1997) argued that "the survival of mimesis, the nonconceptual affinity of the subjectively produced with its unposited other, defines art as a form of knowledge and to that extent as 'rational'" (p. 54). It is in this dynamic that art carries its critical element. It was the decline of autonomously generated art which Adorno came to view as being as a direct consequence of the rise of the culture industry.

Both Adorno and Benjamin came to think of art as a form of language, or having a language-like character, which incites philosophical reflection. This type of thinking was a forerunner to the post-structuralist Jean-François Lyotard's (1971) more recent 'discovery' of the potential liberating tension between discursive (the verbal) and the figural (the visual). Lyotard viewed the unconscious as being associated with the figural and the pre-conscious with language. Art in this context is part of the transgressive and disruptive element in this tension. I will discuss this presently, but in a context of the work of Marcuse and Benjamin who suggest that forms of art, such as surrealism, liberate that critical dimension of art in producing a discomfort or estrangement. These forms of art represent art's own "attempt to rescue the rationality of the negative" (Marcuse, 1964: 67).

The discussion of art as a form of knowledge, and having a language-like character, will culminate in considering the forms of rescuing its own critical dimension, and whether similar forms could be used for *critical* management. In using the term "critical management", I wish to denote forms of thinking that help us see anew that which we have taken-for-granted and may have blinded us to alternative constructions of problems and solutions. Some of the parallels between movements in art and 'schools' of thought in organization studies have featured in this author's previous work (Carr, 1999, 2000a, 2001a; Carr & Zanetti, 2000). On this occasion a more targeted critique is intended and, in particular, a consideration of the field of management itself as merely being part of a culture industry that is intent upon producing, what Adorno (1975) called, "patterned and pre-digested" products with no critical element. In this latter context to speak of critical management would seem an oxymoron.

Having given a sketch of the paper in bold relief, and noted some the direction of the argument, let us examine in a little finer detail some of the work of these scholars associated with the Frankfurt School.

Mimesis and Enigma in Art—Hearing from Benjamin and Adorno

Rainer Rochlitz (1992/1996) argues that "In German aesthetics, avant-garde movements have been interpreted primarily in the light of the concepts elaborated by Benjamin and Adorno. In France, in contrast, whether or not a particular critic favors the avant-garde, he attempts to understand it through Nietzsche" (p. 220). The contrast between the Benjaminian/Adornian orientation to art and aesthetics to that of the Nietzschean orientation, is a contrast that highlights the fundamental working assumption made by the two Frankfurt scholars. Nietzsche insisted art needed to be seen within the sovereignty of its own terms and would suggest that "art tends to set aside any criterion *brought in from* the logical or moral order ...(with) 'truth' (being) a vital illusion and the truth of art a tonic lie" (Rochlitz, 1992/1996: 220; see also Comte-Sponville, 1991/1997: 55-57). Although often drawing upon the work of Nietzsche, on this topic the two Frankfurt scholars had a somewhat different view and, throughout their work, insisted that the "truth content" of art has "not lost its logical and ethical stakes" (Rochlitz, 1992/1996: 220).

Adorno and Benjamin were of the view that art and aesthetics are not some separate order that obey some pure detached aesthetic logic as such, but instead had a co-determined link to the 'otherness' that, putatively, it sought to escape. Art, aesthetics and critical theory had a 'power' to disclose 'truths' about society. In contrast to "shoulder-shrugging aesthetic relativism", Adorno (1970/1997) insisted that "art is directed toward truth, it is not itself immediate truth: to this extent truth is its content. By its relation to truth, art is knowledge; art itself knows truth in that truth emerges through it. As knowledge, however, art is neither discursive nor is its truth the reflection of an object" (p. 282). Of course, Adorno, and his Frankfurt school brethren, reject *any* pretensions to absolute truth and argued that valid knowledge cannot be detached from knowing subjects—knowledge always has to be conceived as mediated through society and has a *dialectic* 'nature' in the interplay of the particular and universal, of the moment and totality (see Carr, 2000b).

For Adorno and Benjamin, art and aesthetics was not only an attempt to represent, but in the representation it had the capacity to transcend that 'rationality' which it was representing. As Adorno (1970/1997: 31) once observed: "The modernity of art lies in its mimetic relation to a petrified and alienated reality. This, and not the denial of that mute reality, is what makes art speak" (see also Rasmussen, 1996: 29). To understand the 'rationality' that art represented and also its transgressive and critical "self-reflexive" 'voice', one needs to appreciate Benjamin and Adorno's conception of *mimesis* and *enigma*. It is these two concepts that are pivotal to their work on art and aesthetics. Indeed, it would not be overstating the case to suggest that these two concepts are the essential scaffolding to how they came to the conclusion that art carried its "truth content" and critical perspective.

The notion of mimesis, although widely used by Adorno and others in the Frankfurt school, was a notion first elaborated upon by their fellow theorist Walter Benjamin. It was this elaboration that shaped the use of the term by others of the Frankfurt school. Benjamin (1933/1999c) suggested that we all have a "mimetic faculty" (mimicry) responsible for producing and perceiving resemblance. While imitation maybe the ultimate form of flattery, and a basic behavior through which we may learn new skills etc., Benjamin (1933/1999b: 698; 1933/1999c: 720) also viewed it as one of our most irresistible impulses. Indeed, Benjamin, along with Adorno, came to think of mimesis as an assimilation of self to other—a type of enactment behavior (Adorno, 1970/1997: 111; Benjamin, 1933/1999c: 720; see also Jay, 1997b: 32; Nicholsen, 1997: 147). This enactment behavior was to anticipate some of the work of Winnicott related to the psychodynamics involved in play (see Winnicott, 1971a, 1971b, 1971c: 41, 1971d: 100, 1971e: 107).

Benjamin (1933/1999c: 720) notes that a child's play is "everywhere permeated by mimetic modes of behavior... The child plays at being not only a shopkeeper or teacher, but also a windmill and a train". Anyone listening to their adolescent offspring trying to sing along with whatever is the top of the hit parade, will soon discover it is not only a matter of getting the words right, you also have to get the right accent to sound like the original! Of course, this behavior is not always reproduced in the same form, i.e., an aural phenomenon imitated aurally. For example, the child who moves through the house as though they were an aeroplane. Here a human being is seeking to imitate a non-human object. Some areas of this imitation, such as flying, are substituted with a behavior that is in another form—in this case, running around the house with outstretched arms. Thus the similarity is not necessarily embodied in the same form. These brief examples cause us to consider, perhaps more deeply, the dimensions of mimesis—not only the issue of the success in producing a likeness, but the more general question, that of: "What is the nature of the link with otherness that is both presupposed and created by imitation?" (Nicholsen, 1997: 138). The ability to produce but *also* perceive resemblance would appear to implicate some form of human mimetic faculty or capacity.

Mimesis and the mimetic faculty, for Benjamin (1933/1999b: 695), in times long gone is different to that of today. In those earlier times, Benjamin points to interest in the cosmic order and divination as the medium through which the reading of correspondence was to occur. Today the system of signs takes the form of language, as Benjamin (1933/1999b) argues:

Language now represents the medium in which objects encounter and come into relation with one another. No longer directly, as they once did in the mind of the augur or priest, but in their essences, in their most transient and delicate substances, even in their aromas. In other words: it is to script and language that clairvoyance has, over the course of history, yielded its old powers (pp. 696-697).

It was the process of producing similarities rather than the object of the similarity that was important for Benjamin (see Nicholsen, 1997: 140)—important, in as much as the mimetic faculty could be noted to exist throughout the course of history. Nicholsen (1997) makes the profound connection of mimesis and self and other, which she notes in the work of Benjamin, and argues: "Language, in short, can mediate the mimetic assimilation of self to other. Words mediate the loss of self as a loss of one's own image, figure, or face. Words could make him like things, Benjamin says, but 'never like my own image'; the child is 'disfigured by likeness' to everything that surrounds him" (p. 143).

Adorno (1970/1997) agreed with these sentiments but suggested that, rather than language, it was art that had become the emergent form of the mimetic impulse. For Adorno (1970/1997), a work of art actually induced mimetic behavior in the viewer (or listener, in the case where he uses the term art in its broader sense to include music, film etc.). He also, however, suggested that art has a rebus-like face—an "enigmatic gaze that it directs at us" (Nicholsen, 1997: 150), which is a non-conceptual but language-like character that incites philosophical reflection. Nicholsen (1997) summarizes Adorno's position extremely well[1] when she says:

The work itself is analogous to a musical score. The recipient—listener, viewer, reader—follows along or mimes the internal trajectories of the work at hand, tracing its internal articulations down the finest nuance... the act of aesthetic understanding is an act whereby the self is assimilated to the other; the subject virtually embodies, in a quasi-sensuous mode, the work, which is other (p. 149).

It is the enigmatic face of the work of art, the enigmatic gaze it directs at us, that incites this philosophical reflection. ... First of all, the work is enigmatic because it is mimetic rather than conceptual. Being nonconceptual, it cannot be unenigmatic, because it cannot have a discursive meaning. Further, it is enigmatic because it lost its purpose when the mimetic migrated from ritual into art; art has become, in Kant's phrase, purposive but without purpose. As Adorno says, art cannot answer the question, "What are you for?"

The enigmatic quality implies otherness as well as affinity. It requires distance if it is to be perceived. The experiential understanding of art that is gained through mimetic assimilation to the work does not have this kind of distance. It is trapped inside the work, so to speak, and accordingly cannot do justice to it (pp. 149-150; see also Adorno, 1970/1997: 119-131).

For Adorno, all autonomously generated artworks are enigmas in as much as they have a capacity to sustain this discrepancy between projected images and their actuality. Carrying similarity yet difference at the same time: "Artworks say something and in the same breath conceal it..." (Adorno, 1970/1997: 120; see also

Held, 1980/1995: 82, 83, 88-89). At one point Adorno (1970/1997) added to this dynamic and argued that "the survival of mimesis, the nonconceptual affinity of the subjectively produced with its unposited other, defines art as a form of knowledge and to that extent as 'rational' "(p. 54). Art is everywhere engaged in a dialectic with reason in its various forms: as cognition, construction, technique, spiritualization, objectification etc. (see Nicholsen, 1997: 148). Art overcomes the constraining and unreflective nature of rationality through the very act of expression of non-identity with itself. The 'truth-value' of art arises from this ability to sustain "a discrepancy between its projected images (concepts) of nature and humankind, and its objects' actuality" (see Held, 1980/1995: 82). These were the dynamics in which art was considered to carry its critical perspective. It was also the decline in this autonomous art that Adorno saw as the flip-side of the rise of the culture industry which will be discussed presently. It is to this 'latent' critical content carried by art to which I now turn our attention.

The Critical Content of Art: Hearing from Benjamin, Marcuse and Adorno on Surrealism

The notion that *works of art return our gaze in a manner so as to induce critical reflection*, was something that some of the Frankfurt School thought was particularly well exemplified in the work of the surrealists. Benjamin and Marcuse, and a little less so Adorno[2], used the *example* of surrealism, as a somewhat 'exaggerated'[3] case, to illustrate how the critical content of autonomous art gets played out in a dialectic manner assumed in critical theory. Benjamin and Marcuse found that the body of work by the surrealists engendered an opportunity to see the world anew. The variety of techniques developed by the surrealists in writing, poetry, painting, theatre and film were intended to create new associations and overthrow the usual linear correspondence of objects and 'logical'/ familiar associations.

It was the paintings by de Chirico during 1911-1917 that inspired some of the early work of the surrealists. Indeed, Breton (1927/1965: 83) saw the work of de Chirico as reflecting the founding philosophy of surrealism. In some senses De Chirico might be considered to be a surrealist, but his work did in fact preface both the formal declaration of surrealism by Breton in 1924 (see Breton, 1924/1969) and a subsequent movement of the surrealists into the medium of painting. De Chirico, like some of the 'officially' declared surrealist painters that followed, e.g., Magritte, Dali, Delvaux, and Toyen, questioned the familiar identity of objects by faithfully reproducing them but placing them in unfamiliar settings and using such unfamiliar associations to produce a kind of poetic strangeness. The rich mimetic and the enigmatic mixture of the work. The shock of the juxtaposition of objects in unfamiliar association elicited unforeseen affinities between objects and, perhaps, unexpected emotion and sensations in the observer. As Breton more generally observed: "the external object had broken with its customary surroundings, its component parts were somehow emancipated from the object in such a way as to set up entirely new relationships with other elements, escaping from the principle of reality while still drawing upon the real plane (*and overthrowing the idea of correspondence*)" (italics added) (1927/1965: 83[4]).

It is important to recognize that the intent of the surrealist was to break with the 'language' of correspondence of that rationalism and logic that had, in their view, led to the atrocities of WW1. Civilization seemed to have lost its justification and new ways of thinking were needed that were more *authentic* and particularly not infected by bourgeois society. This orientation is nicely captured in the words of the surrealist Patrick Waldberg (1965/1997) when he observes that surrealism is:

> *A distrust of rationalism and formal conventions (which were worshipped at that time by the representatives of the avant-garde) prompted the young men towards the exploration of the realm of the unconscious and the dream. They were seeking what might be called 'the language of the soul', that is, the expression—stripped of all logical device—of the profound 'me' in its nakedness* (p. 13).

Surrealism actually had its beginnings in the written word but, it soon became associated with visual art for which it is probably more commonly known today. In their efforts to transcend rationality and linear thinking, the very early surrealists developed some specific techniques and approaches. One technique, the use of *dreams* or inducing a dream-like state to give the unconscious unimpeded passage, was inspired by the work of Freud (1900/1986: 769), who once said that dreams were the royal road to knowledge of the unconscious. The importance of dreams to the surrealists was such that Breton (1924/1969: 14) specifically contrasted it with reality and suggested that he "believed in the future resolution of these two states, dream and reality, which are seemingly so contradictory, into a kind of absolute reality, a *sur-reality*". Other techniques and approaches developed by the early surrealists included: the *exquisite corpse* (stringing together of arbitrary chosen phrases by different poets unaware of what preceded or followed); and, *automatic writing* (writing quickly without control, self-censorship, or thought for the outcome in terms of literary merit, making free associations as they seem to flow).

When it came to surrealism as an expression in the visual arts, the artists also experimented to try and produce further techniques that transcended rationality and the control and presence of the "author". Some of these techniques included *automatic drawing and painting* (similar to automatic writing but in this case not trying to control the hand—an extreme version of this was draw with one's eyes closed); *decalcomania* (placing a sheet of paper with wet paint onto another sheet of paper and then separating them to reveal 'patterns'); *coulage* (paint drippings onto a canvas); *collage* (reassembly of objects on a canvas without concern for how they might be arranged and juxtaposed) and *frottage*. Breton (1948/1965) also insisted that the "*exquisite corpse*" could be used in drawing and suggested it was "an infallible way of holding the critical intellect in abeyance, and of fully liberating the mind's *metaphorical activity*" (italics added) (p. 95). In the drawn version, "players" took turns adding portions of the drawing. The first person might draw the head, with two lines protruding for the neck. The paper was then folded and passed to the second player, who added the torso, with lines protruding across folds for the arms and legs, and so on. The point of the "*play*" was both collective and automatic: the unleashing of the "marvelous" or non-rational, and the production of a work that could not have been produced by a single player acting alone (Caws, 1997).

Marcuse and Benjamin both viewed surrealism as producing discomfort, turmoil, shock and/or emotional disturbance and in so doing was a form of sociocultural critique. The shock induced through the juxtaposition and dissociation of the familiar in unfamiliar settings was particularly resonant with their ideas associated with dialectics. They came to view this discomfort and shock in a manner similar to that captured by Bertolt Brecht in his idea of an "estrangement-effect". Citing the words of Brecht, Marcuse (1964) explains the effect in the following manner.

To teach what the contemporary world really is behind the ideological and material veil, and how it can be changed, the theater must break the spectator's identification with the events on the stage. Not empathy and feeling, but distance and reflection are required. The "estrangement-effect" (Verfremdungseffekt) is to produce this dissociation in which the world can be recognized as what it is. "The things of everyday life are lifted out of the realm of the self-evident... That which is 'natural' must assume the features of the extraordinary. Only in this manner can the laws of cause and effect reveal themselves" (Brecht, 1957; Marcuse, 1964: 67).

Marcuse further argued, using literature as a specific example, that the estrangement-effect "is not superimposed on literature. It is rather literature's own answer to the threat of total behaviorism—the attempt to rescue the rationality of the negative" (p. 67). Amongst other things, for Marcuse, the estrangement-effect was part of a "great refusal" to one-dimensionality.

For Marcuse, the limitations that were being imposed upon freedom and happiness by a domineering and repressive society had an antidote in the liberation of imagination. It was the enslavement of imagination that aided and abetted a social amnesia as to how the present sociocultural arrangements came into being—a social reification, and at the same time robbed us of thinking of alternative possibilities. It was in this context that Marcuse cites Breton's *First Manifesto of Surrealism*:

To reduce imagination to slavery—even if one's so-called happiness is at stake—means to violate all that one finds in one's inmost self of ultimate justice. Imagination alone tells me what can be (Marcuse, 1956/1998: 149 citing Breton, 1924/1969: 4-5).

Both Benjamin and Marcuse saw an affinity between the surrealists' production of the estrangement-effect and the mode of critical thought championed by the Frankfurt School scholars, i.e., dialectics. This affinity was such that Benjamin (1929/1997b) argued that surrealism needed to be perceived dialectically in order to appreciate its purpose and contribution and, in particular, to understand that "we penetrate the mystery only to the degree that we recognize it in the everyday world, by virtue of a *dialectical optic* (italics added) that perceives the everyday as impenetrable, the impenetrable as everyday" (p. 237).

The dialectic optic is used in its Hegelian sense[5]. The estrangement that comes from contradiction, paradox and irony are the necessary reflective opportunities in which juxtaposition aids dialectical self-consciousness. Indeed, in Aragon's 'anti-novel' *Paris Peasant*, this surrealist argues that "reality is the apparent absence of contradiction. The wondrous is contradiction appearing in the real" (Aragon, 1926/1971: 166). Benjamin (1929/1997b: 227) came to describe this wondrous revelation carried in surrealism as "profane illumination". He also reinforced that the act of reflection in the medium that is the work of art and the link to philosophy, when he observed that "all genuine works have their siblings in the realm of philosophy" and that our task in understanding the work of art is to reveal the "virtual possibility of formulating the work's truth content" (Benjamin, 1922/1997a: 333, 334).

For Benjamin and Marcuse, in the surrealist movement the estrangement-effect becomes an artistic-political reflective device only to the extent that the estrangement can be maintained "to produce the shock which may bare the true relationship between the two worlds and languages: the one being the positive negation of the other" (Marcuse, circa unknown/1993: 187). Marcuse warns that, in the past, intellectual oppositions to the mainstream became impotent and ineffective because the estrangement-effect was, in effect, disarmed by the assimilating mechanisms of the prevailing order. He argues in *Aragon* , for example:

The avant-gardistic negation was not negative enough. The destruction of all content was itself not destroyed. The formless form was kept intact, aloof from the universal contamination. The form itself was stabilized as a new content, and thus came to share the fate of all contents: it was absorbed by the market (Marcuse, circa unknown/1993: 182).

Thus the estrangement-effect can only be maintained to the extent that it continues to reveal the prevailing order in its opposition and (simultaneously) the opposition in the prevailing order—that is, to the extent that it maintains a dialectical tension. The opposition between antagonistic spheres, is a dynamic conceived as the mediation of one through the other (see Adorno, 1970/1997: 44-45). This, of course, is the dialectic optic that Benjamin argued was crucial to the understanding of surrealism[6].

The dialectic dynamic inherent in the surrealist movement was also noted by Adorno, particularly in the context of throwing the spotlight on those aspects of social life that functionalism neglects, obscures and/or seeks to remove from our vision. He expresses this view succinctly when he says:

[Surrealist paintings] ... gathered together what functionalism covers with taboos because it betrays reality as reification and the irrational in its rationality. Surrealism recaptures what functionalism denies to man; the distortions demonstrate what the taboo did to the desired. Thus surrealism rescues the obsolete—an album of idiosyncrasies where the claim for happiness evaporates that which the technified world refuses to man [Theodor W. Adorno, "Rückblickend auf den Surrealismus", in Noten zur Literatur. (Berlin-Frankfurt, Suhrkamp, 1958: 160)—Cited in Marcuse, 1964: 70].

Adorno (1970/1997) was to remark, more generally, that art could not be reduced to "the unquestionable polarity of the mimetic and the constructive, as if this were an invariant formula" but what "was fruitful in modern art was what gravitated toward one of the extremes, not what sought to mediate between the two" (p. 44). This line of thought leads Adorno to make a more general point about dialectics, when he states that "the dialectic of these elements is similar to dialectical logic, in that *each pole realizes itself only in the other, and not in some middle ground*" (italics added) (p. 44).

In the *Dialectic of Enlightenment,* although not adopting these words, it was the dialectic tension and the maintenance of some estrangement that Adorno and Horkheimer (1944/1997) had concern, in the face of the culture industry. They despaired at how the culture industry had assimilated the arts into a world of advertising and kitsch[7] and in this process of objectification had repressed (neutralized) art's critical knowledge content. To further understand the critical knowledge element and the language-like quality of art and aesthetics, it is instructive to very briefly consider some of the contours of Adorno and Horkheimer's view about the development of what they dubbed the "culture industry".

Art as Part of the Culture Industry: Hearing from Adorno (& Horkheimer)[8]

Adorno and Horkheimer (1944/1997) in their book *Dialectic of Enlightenment*[9], in a chapter entitled "The culture industry: Enlightenment as mass deception", suggest that 'art'[10] and manual labor have become structurally divided. They viewed capitalism[11] as engendering a new form of domination. The power of the ruling classes was being reproduced through a form of ideological hegemony; it was established primarily through the rule of consent, and mediated via cultural institutions such as schools, the family, churches and mass media. It was in this context that Adorno and Horkheimer argued that culture, like everything else in capitalist society, had been transformed into an object. This objectification resulted in both the repression of the critical elements in its form and content, but also represented a negation of critical thought. As Adorno (1975) was to remark:

Culture in the true sense, did not simply accommodate itself to human beings; ... it always simultaneously raised a protest against the petrified relations under which they lived, thereby honoring them. Insofar as culture becomes wholly assimilated to and integrated into those petrified relations, human beings are once more debased (p. 13).

Culture had, metaphorically, become another industry producing commodities, which had little or no critical function. Adorno (1975: 14) was to clarify that "the expression 'industry' is not to be taken literally. It refers to the standardization of the thing itself—such as the Western, familiar to every moviegoer—and to the rationalization of distribution techniques ... (and) not strictly to the production process". To paraphrase Adorno in a number of his works (see also Held, 1980/1995: 94; Rocco, 1994: 87), music, art, film were essentially, aimed at a passive, passionless and uncritical reception, which it induces through the production of "patterned and pre-digested" products. The culture industry anticipates individual consumer 'need'. The images and messages that are commercially produced are largely *mimetic* of the broader sociopolitical relations. The criteria of merit for these products was perverted, according to Adorno and Horkheimer (1944/1997: 124), as it was judged by the amount of "conspicuous consumption".

Positivist rationality, the manipulation and suppression of critical imagination, were embodied in the images and messages produced by the culture industry—an industry so reductionist that culture was mere amusement. The structural division between work and 'art' (read culture) was such that culture was to be the vehicle of escape from the boredom, drudgery and powerlessness inherent in mechanized work processes. Culture had, instead, become an extension of that same world of work. In the words of Adorno and Horkheimer (1944/1997: 137):

Amusement under late capitalism is the prolongation of work[12]. It is sought after as an escape from the mechanized work process, and to recruit strength in order to be able to cope with it again. But at the same time mechani-

zation has such power over a man's leisure and happiness, and so profoundly determines the manufacture of amusement goods, that his experiences are inevitably after-images of the work process itself. The ostensible content is merely faded foreground; what sinks in is the automatic succession of standardized operations (for a similar critique, see also Marcuse, 1956/1998, 1964, 1968).

Nowhere was Adorno and Horkheimer's criticism of the culture industry greater, and more illustrative, than in the realm of art. Scathing as to what art had become, Adorno and Horkheimer suggested that *art had not simply been turned into a commodity, but from the outset was conceived of as an item for sale to a market.* In an idiom of style, art and advertising had merged as cultural products with perhaps the ultra-realism of Andy Warhol's Campbell Soup painting saying it all (see Giroux, 1983: 21). The one dimensional society, highlighted by Marcuse (1964), is a world that collapses the distinction between what is and what might otherwise be possible and, at the same time, reifies—serving to encourage a social amnesia as to the ontology of such a world. The aesthetic character of art that brings enjoyment and entertainment now, simultaneously, serves to pacify and, in many instances, has been turned over as an instrument to aid in the promotion and acquisition of commodities. The 'prevailing' interpretation of reality gets reproduced and reinforced such that the reconciliation of alienated individuals with society occurs through a process of identification of the latter with the former, as Held (1980/1995) cogently observes:

The 'plots', the 'goodies', the 'heroes' rarely suggest anything other than identification with the existing form of social relations. There is passion in movies, radio broadcasting, popular music and magazines, but it is usually passion for identity (between whole and part, form and content, subject and object). The products of the culture industry can be characterized by standardization and pseudo-individu-

alization. It is these qualities which distinguish them from autonomous art (p. 94).

Art had been robbed of its ability to suggest alternative possibilities to a world in which it now seemed to merely act as a mirror. To reverse a Kantian expression, in the words of Adorno and Horkheimer (1944/1997: 158; see also Adorno, 1970/1997: 139); "The principle of idealistic aesthetics—purposefulness without a purpose—reverses the scheme of things to which bourgeois art conforms socially: purposelessness for the purpose declared by the market". Art had been neutralized into a mere object of contemplation[13]. Art had become part of the culture industry that promoted, and sought to have assumed, intellectual and social conformity.

Management and Organization Studies: Taking Lessons from the World of Art?

Having heard from some of the Frankfurt School scholars on the matter of art as a form of knowledge and its language-like character, the question arises: "How might the work of these scholars provide us with a valuable optic through which to more deeply *understand* and *reflexively explore* management and organization studies?" I would suggest the work of these scholars, on the matter of art, is helpful in a number of ways which are perhaps most conveniently addressed under three subheadings.

1. Management and Organization Studies: Has it Become a Culture Industry?

In 1997 a book was published, written by Gibson Burrell, entitled *Pandemonium: Towards a retro-organization theory*. In the same year David Farmer (1997a) made a conference presentation entitled "Public administration discourse as (Heraclitean, Derridean) play: Does it pay to play?" (see also Farmer, 1998). Both of these prominent contributors to the organization discourses were independently voicing a disillusionment and seeking to 'extract' themselves from the mode of thinking that had characterized these discourses. Both of them had turned to post modernism which, at the time, I interpreted (see Carr, 1997; Carr & Zanetti, 1998) as, unknowingly, entering the realm of surrealism—more of that connection, of postmodernism and surrealism, in a moment. The core of their disillusionment appeared to be the shallowness or superficial 'nature' of the discourse and, in particular, linear thinking. Burrell (1997) expressed his disillusionment and frustration with the discourse throughout the book, both explicitly and implicitly. Early in his tome, in addressing those in the field that he expected to be his readers, he suggested that if his book were a video, "decidedly not for public viewing", it would show "that we're swimming in deep shit" (p. 4). Burrell (1997) goes on to make the following argument as to why he holds this view, saying:

The pressures to carry out work of an empiricist kind, to make this research relevant to a managerial audience and to play for good and instant feedback from teaching our clients, places tremendous pressures towards conservatism on lecturing staff (p. 4).

To put this comment in even greater context, it must be remembered that this was the 'same' Burrell who once joined with Morgan (Burrell & Morgan, 1979) and posed that most unKuhnian rendering of paradigms. You know that Burrell—the 2x2 typology in which 'human nature' became part of their strange brew of unproblematic oppositional dimensionality, and who talked of being confined to 'cells' in a context of incommensurability. In *Pandemonium*, this was clearly a different Burrell (1997) now observes that he "now leaves the equally sized rooms he has been stalking" (p. 25).

The work of Adorno and Horkheimer (1944/1997) might suggest that Burrell and Farmer, and of course others, are at one level expressing the pressures associated with a *culture industry*. Using the optic of the culture industry one might ask for some reflexivity—to inquire as to whether, both in the content and teaching methodology, as well as in research, the field in which we toil is simply another culture industry? For example, we often, jokingly, refer to MBAs as undergraduate management degrees for engineers. Carried in the joke is, perhaps, a hint of a larger story, a story that has something to say more generally about the field. MBAs and many other degrees in management and administration could be seen, very much, as commodities to be purchased from a marketplace. Commodities that give a superficial understanding of the subject matter. Burrell (1997: 27) remarks upon this superficiality when he invites some readers to exit his book as early as page twenty six. He refers to these 'scholars' as "being content with 'Heathrow Organization Theory' and its practitioners (e.g., Handy, 1994)". He then distinguishes his own volume by distancing it from the "Handy pocket theory with all its superficiality, ease of travel, liberal humanistic stance, techno-babble language and fundamentally conservative political leaning ... (and) all that consultancy-speak" (Burrell, 1997: 27).

Recalling the summary in the last section of this paper about what art had become, the question remains: "Has the teaching, research and discourse in management and organization studies become another culture industry, aimed at a passive, passionless and uncritical reception, which it induces through the production of patterned and pre-digested products?" The answer, for many of us, is a resounding YES. The work of Adorno and Horkheimer (1944/1997) has provided the basis to pose this fundamental question and in doing so has given us a basis for some reflexivity. For the scholars of the Frankfurt School, art is certainly a form of knowledge. It also represents "a kind of rationality that contains a certain 'non-rational' element that eludes the instrumental form" (Rasmussen, 1996: 29). Art's non-rational element gives it the power to go beyond instrumental rationality. For Adorno (1970/1997: 79) "capitalist society hides and disavows precisely this irrationality, whereas art does not". In this context, earlier it was observed, and it bears repeating, that:

Adorno (1970/1997) insisted that "art is directed toward truth, it is not itself immediate truth: to this extent truth is its content. By its relation to truth, art is knowledge; art itself knows truth in that truth emerges through it. As knowledge, however, art is neither discursive nor is its truth the reflection of an object" (p. 282). Of course, Adorno, and his Frankfurt school brethren, reject any pretensions to absolute truth and argued that valid knowledge cannot be detached from knowing subjects—knowledge always has to be conceived as mediated through society and has a dialectic 'nature' in the interplay of the particular and universal, of the moment and totality (see Carr, 2000b).

In seeking to liberate ourselves, and the discourse more generally, from the culture industry, a dialectic optic would cause us to more reflexively consider what our 'own' discourse offers us as knowledge. The critical dimension of our gaze is still within 'the work', in as much, as we can see the superficiality and note the contradictions and ruptures in the 'images' that is our discourse—the field's own mimesis and enigma dynamic. More than this, a dialectic optic would have our gaze upon knowledge itself as being an object of study in a twofold sense. In one sense we can examine our 'knowledge' in a context of understanding its social function, that is, the manner in which it legitimates certain practices and structures. At the same time, our 'knowledge' can be analyzed "to reveal through its arrangement, words, structure and style those unintentional truths that contain 'fleeting images'" (Giroux, 1983: 30) of other possibilities.

2. The Contemporary Evocation of Surrealism in Management and Organization Studies

I noted earlier that prominent organization theorists such as Burrell (1997) and Farmer (1997a, 1997b, 1998), as well as others, had sought to extract themselves from "linearity" and totalizing "logic" (Burrell, 1997: 27) by adopting a postmodern perspective. I interpreted this, at the time (see Carr, 1997; Carr & Zanetti, 1998), as, 'unknowingly', entered the realm of surrealism. Indeed, as my review of Burrell's work was being published, in which I made this connection, Farmer's aforementioned conference paper came out in a special issue of the journal *Public Voices*, edited by Farmer (1997b) himself. This special issue focused upon postmodernism and public administration. The cover of this special issue featured a surrealist work, a reproduction of the Rene Magritte's painting "The Blank Signature". Farmer comments in his introduction, that this painting makes the point that "reality extends beyond conscious rationality" (p. 8). I was left to ponder if he, and or any of the other authors in this special issue, had also ever considered any possible deeper connections between postmodernism and surrealism?

The contours of that original argument, that much of postmodernist thought was a contemporary evocation of surrealism, is an argument that bears revisiting in the context of this paper[14]. It is an argument, that if sustained, also provides some clues as to how the analysis of surrealism by the scholars of the Frankfurt School, discussed earlier in this paper, has implications for the management and organization discourse. This is, again, an attempt to learn from the world of art and those who have noted a transgressive and critical 'voice' of art.

In the context of explaining how some the Frankfurt School scholars viewed surrealism as somewhat of an exemplar of the manner in which art carried its critical element or content, it was earlier noted that the surrealists sought to transcend rationality and linear logic. To achieve this objective, it was also noted that the surrealists developed techniques such as: the exquisite corpse; automatic writing/drawing/painting; dream work; decalcomania; coulage; collage; frottage; and others of a playful kind. Postmodernists appear to have taken a similar path. Their fundamental orientation is also to transcend rationality, linear thinking, and the 'author'. The central and recurrent themes of postmodernism are that '*its all in the text*' and the importance of *the death-of-the-subject.* Also, postmodernists generally embrace the early poststructuralist view that 'truth' is merely a construction of language (see Lyotard, 1984: xxiii). Moreover, the human as a subject is likewise simply part of that text, nothing more than a transient epiphenomenon of a specific and local cultural discourse.

Derrida (1976) insists *il n'y a pas de hors-texte* (p. 158), i.e., there is nothing outside of the text. Postmodernists ask us to consider the text without relation to any fixed referents, whether those referents be historical or metaphysical. For Derrida words gain "their" meaning from their relationship to other words that may be presented at the same time, i.e., in the same written or spoken discourse and/or from their implied relationship to other words that do not appear in that discourse. It is this "play of difference" that is at the heart of how language needs to be examined. Derrida similarly insists the text itself is a bearer of a statement, whose truth is problematic, as its "elements" have a fluid rather than fixed meaning. It is in this context that the self has no referential status other than the text, and the hallmarks of Enlightenment—knowing, naming, and emancipation—become problematic.

As noted earlier, the surrealists were extremely sensitive to exactly the same issues that Derrida raised, sharing a distaste for representation as it signified mastery ["odius supremacy" (Breton, 1927/1965: 81)]—whether that representation were political, social, linguistic, or cultural in origin. For the surrealist visual artists it was the interplay of absence and presence [akin to Derrida's *écriture*] that was relied on to produce a kind of poetic strangeness. Its signification was not through everyday meaning, but through the impact of disturbing the everyday associations, and thus problematizing what seemed to be real. The faith in one's 'eyes' was challenged. For example, the idea of overthrowing correspondence, through the placing of familiar objects in unfamiliar associations and settings, was intended to inspire an anti-representational outcome in the observer—but it was the observer who was to make the 'meaning', not the artist [akin to the postmodernists 'death-of-the-subject/author']. Sarup (1993) makes a parallel comment in respect of post-structuralists/postmodernists, arguing that "broadly speaking the signified is demoted and the signifier made dominant. This means there is no one-to-one correspondence between propositions and reality" (p. 3). A similar comment is made by Rosenau (1992) when she points out that "reader-oriented postmodernism implies that meaning originates not in the production of a text (with the author), but in its reception (by the reader)" (p. 37). These intentions are exactly those of the surrealists.

In postmodernist formulations the self or individual has no referential status other than the text. The self becomes figured and reconfigured as a textual creation. This is such a fundamental theme of postmodern thinking that one writer concludes "the connection between ... thinkers and theories of postmodernity has mainly to do with their announcements of the 'death of man' (Foucault), or the 'death of the subject' (Derrida), or the 'death of the author' (Barthes)" (Kumar, 1995: 129). The individual is a part of the text and not first and foremost its subject. Indeed, we find the parallel in the surrealist movement in as much as Breton (1930/1969), at one stage, even contemplated encouraging surrealists to remove their name from 'their' works as he feared that being able to identify the 'author' would color interpretation and too closely tie them to the world. At one point he declares that "the approval of the public is to be avoided like the plague" (p. 177). Under the subheading "I ask for the profound, the veritable occultation of surrealism", he says: "I proclaim, in this matter, the right of absolute severity. No concessions to the world, and no grace" (pp. 177 and 178). The nihilism of the surrealists, i.e., the disdain and rejection of a belief of values, which is also so characteristic of the postmodernists[15], is openly declared in the earlier writing of Breton. The rejection of modernism, and what it represents, was an early touchstone for the surrealists along with absenting the knowing subject.

For many postmodernists, individuality and consciousness are conceived of as verbally grounded experiences where self-awareness can only be realized through hearing oneself and being acknowledged by others through discourse, "man [sic] is decentered; the individual subject is dissolved into linguistic structures and ensembles of relations" (Kvale, 1992: 40). Thus, like the surrealists, the postmodernists seek to transcend or absent the 'author'.

The similarity in orientation of postmodernist formulations with those of the surrealists suggest a close affinity. In many ways, it should not be at all surprising to find that the 'techniques' used in the service of such an orientation should also be similar. If, in the interests of brevity and immediate relevance, we concentrate on those in the discourse of organization studies and management that had championed postmodernism, we gain a rapid appreciation of the specific form that these have taken in our discourse. Our aforementioned Gibson Burrell (1997) and David Farmer (1997a, 1997b, 1998), for example, have asked us to become *playful* by engaging questions such as—"what if it wasn't like this but the opposite?" They suggest that it is through *a clash-of-opposites* that we may transcend the logic and rationality of the day. In Farmer's case, the "play of irony" is particularly viewed as important in considering, for example, public administration as a language game. Burrell's playfulness is a little more elaborate.

Burrell's book is a medieval tale that is full of despair, images of death and decay, and is designed to shock our sensibilities. In a Hegel-versus-Nietzsche view of history, crudely summarized as teleology versus genealogy, Burrell has taken the side of Nietzsche. Nietzsche (1901/1968) rejected totalizing forms of analysis and instead advocated an approach that looks at the present and moves back in time until a difference is found. Burrell appears to have chosen the medieval period as it represented a time where the contrast between the aspects of the present he is so discomforted by are so different from the past. He declares that Pandemonium does not represent "an argument, or a thesis or a story. It is a ludibrium—a playful toying with ideas—more than anything else and contains hidden meanings of which I am not aware" (1997: 28). Burrell also formats the book in a way to try to escape linearity and conventional logic and induce free association. The formatting is such that page numbering is not conventional. The numbers are neither at the top or bottom of the page but indeed on the side of the page often flanked by an arrow to give the reader an indication of where to read next. There is a "dual carriageway in which text across the top half of the page moving from left to right 'meets' text moving from right to left across the bottom half of the page. Pages have a central reservation which it is always dangerous to cross" (Burrell, 1997: 2). This intertwining of form and content, that Burrell employs, was the very essence of the techniques beginning with De Chirico, later in the exquisite corpse and automatic writing, to also inspire free association and thus move beyond the constraints of conventional logic.

In addition to *playfulness*, the *clash-of-opposites* and *intertwining of form and content*, other 'surrealist' techniques can be noted in the work of the group of writers who claim, or invoke, the insights of postmodernists in the organization discourse. These well established writers have been advocating what, at first glance, seems to be using the fantastic to elucidate assumptions and neglected visions. These techniques have included: *deconstruction* (an introspective activity that seeks to unsettle the taken for granted meaning and assumptions of a text by using the text against itself, e.g., by *erasing* one word/concept, and substituting its 'opposite' also by scanning the text for contradictions and disruptions in the words, expressions, and ideas that are used and by so doing, putatively, exposing a text's logocentrism); and, *metaphoricality* (the use of metaphors not just to capture a general idea but to be used as a tool to explore thinking of organizations *as if*, e.g., as if they are organisms—using this metaphor we may consider the issues as organizational health, decision centres, the existence and role of feedback, homeostasis, and the like, aspects that are, putatively, hidden or obscured from our everyday vision and consciousness).

Not to labor the point, the parallels of these techniques with those of the surrealists, are summarized in Appendix A . If for the moment it is accepted that surrealism, in the form of a contemporary evocation postmodernism, in both its orientation and techniques, has permeated the discourse of organization studies and management, then are their lessons to learnt from the appreciation of the surrealist art movement? The work of the Frankfurt School scholars, outlined earlier in this paper, is instructive here. It was noted, for both Benjamin and Marcuse surrealism needed to be interpreted dialectically in order to appreciate its purpose and contribution. It creates an estrangement-effect, and provides "profane illumination", to the degree that it continues to reveal the prevailing order in its opposition and (simultaneously) the opposition in the prevailing order—a dialectic tension. This estrangement-effect is, as Marcuse (1964: 67) argued, not something that we can impose upon our own field, but is an endogenous reaction to rescue that 'rationality' of the negative. The problem here is that oppositions are all too easily absorbed into the prevailing discourse. In the case of surrealism, as was noted in an early work describing an 'exhibition' of surrealism held at the Galerie des Beaux-Arts, in Paris on the 17th January 1938:

... by 1938, when the exhibition was held, images and devices from the visual portion of Surrealism had already begun to be appropriated by advertisers and marketers. Dali, for example, was designing perfume bottles shaped like torsos. Miro's biomorphic fantasies were beginning to influence furnishings and interiors. Rather than announcing a revolution, the 1938 exhibition seemed more a display of radical chic about to cross the threshold into textbook history. Reviewers accused the Surrealists of seeming to take risks while actually being disengaged, and lamented "one more revolution that fades into that which it wishes to overturn" (Sawin, 1995: 8; Carr & Zanetti, 2000: 915).

Similarly, G. Garfield Crimmins in an the recent wonderfully evocative, humorous and erotic journey in a book entitled *The Republic of Dreams: A Reverie* (1998), takes us to the 'land' of dreams called the Rêverian Republic. During this time-travel, we are treated to surrealist images and provided with the "Visitor's Guide to la République de Rêves" in which it is noted:

Recently discovered documents in which the original Rêverians referred to themselves as "Rondomites" suggests a connection with the Randomites, a society of nonlinear thinkers active in the 1920s. Their membership was international, as was their persecution and suppression by linear thinkers of the period. By 1938, nothing more was heard of them and all traces of their activities had vanished (p. 28).

The recent postmodernist formulations in the organization and management discourse, seem also set to become mainstreamed and commercialized which will fracture the dialectic. The terminology of postmodernism, such as 'postmodern' and 'deconstruction' seems to be heading in the same direction as the way in which the overuse of the word 'paradigm' has left it devoid of its original meaning. One of the lessons to be learnt, would seem to be, that the field itself needs to on its guard against the decontextualizing of concepts and allowing a variety of 'chain-saws' to be applied to the theoretics. Only by caring for the integrity and authenticity of streams of thought, can we take advantage of how that estrangement-effect helps in the re-presentation of previously-accepted truths and social conditions. In similar vein and unknowingly reflecting the Marcuse (1964: 67) cite of Brecht's explanation of the "estrangement-effect" that was used earlier in this paper, Cooper and Burrell (1988) note in a passing reference to the significance of the work of Foucault that:

> *...the auratic dimension appears as a form of 'estrangement' in which the normal and familiar come to be seen in a novel and sometimes disturbing way. In order to see the ordinary with a fresh vision, we have to make it 'extraordinary', i.e., to break the habits of organized routine and see the world 'as though for the first time'; it is necessary to free ourselves of normalized ways of thinking that blind us to the strangeness of the familiar* (p. 101).

The group of writers who have advanced a post-modernist view in the discourse of organization studies and management have, unknowingly, entered the realms of surrealism. If this argument was indulged a little further, what if writers were to literally adopt a surrealist orientation and seek to develop new forms and manifestations of surrealist 'techniques'. Such a development would seem to advance the cause of enhancing "fresh vision". Equally, it might also be instructive to look at other 'surrealist movements' in other fields to understand and explore new approaches.

For example, it has very recently been suggested that in the field of literature, magic realism might be similarly productive (see Carr, 2001b). Magic realism, as the name implies, is a form of representation that juxtaposes reality and fantasy. Although originally a form of art, it gains its more elaborate evocation in writing of a group of writers that reside in Latin America, most notably Gabriel

Garcia Márquez, Octavio Paz and Carlos Fuentes, These authors create narratives in which the realistic elements of the text are undermined by reference to events that have not occurred and situations that are impossible. In his introduction to a volume of *Latin American Stories*, Fuentes (1998) remarks that as a story writer:

you are ... expected to construct your stories in one of two ways: in either a 'realistic' or a 'fantastic' mode. I, for one, have always tried to avoid this stark choice by recalling the lesson of Balzac and particularly The Wild Ass's Skin. The novelist who wished to be the public notary of French social classes 'carried a whole society' in his head, but also carried ghosts, myths, fears, unexplainable occurrences and a wild ass's skin that fulfils your desires but shrinks every time it gives, until, at the end, it takes life from the hapless owner and disappears (p. xii).

Some historians (see Gonzalez-Echevarría, 1977) have suggested that the origins of magic realism are distinctly Latin American, pointing to the Cuban novelist Alejo Carpentíer's work *The Kingdom of This World* (1949) in which there is reference to "lo real-maravilloso" (the marvellous-real, as was noted earlier in this paper, the surrealists also talked of their own work as unleashing the "marvellous"—see Spector, 1997). Carpentíer, in this book, describes his reaction to what he sees as the fantastic and brutal history of Haiti. He argues that the "marvellous" is a feature of life in Latin America, and the Caribbean, that cannot be authentically reproduced by the realism of a Dickens. Thus, magic realist, postmodernist, or surrealist, all liberate the "marvelous" through what the Frankfurt School detected as that vital quality of a 'medium' to carry similarity and difference at the same time. This quality not only needs to be understood, but the dynamics of assimilation mechanisms also revealed.

3. The Sissociation of Sensibilities

A third issue for the field of organization studies and management, that I believe immediately suggests itself from the work of the Frankfurt scholars on the matter of art, relates to a range of philosophical issues. In particular, those issues related to what the poet T. S. Eliot dubbed the "dissociation of sensibilities" (see Carr, 2000b). It seems almost self-evident that modernism itself has encouraged a separation of our forms of knowledge within the social science. Each phenomena, including that of our everyday life, we are encouraged to examine through a multiplicity of specialist lenses. This differentiation has been accompanied with a regime that encourages: scientism; the realists idea that something is mind-independent; and, pervasive forms of "dualisms (nature vs. culture, mind vs. matter) that have served to valorize an abstract idealism at the expense of an embodied, practical rationality" (see Gardiner, 2000: 11). Different knowledge-forms, the abstractions, the hierarchy in the knowledge-forms that gives primacy to metaphysical reason, and dualisms—all, have splintered and substituted for 'real life' and negate critical function.

The work of the Frankfurt scholars, in their critical examination of art and aesthetics, alerts us to some ways in which the issue of 'truth' might be explored in a much more reflexive manner. Of course, it is all too easy to confuse truth and knowledge, but these Frankfurt scholars have teased-out that relationship. Their work leads us to the discovery that the issue is not one of objective truth, but one of some transparency over how we come to hold the conclusions that we do. What logic, reason and other mediated pathways did we use (consciously and unconsciously guided), in coming to "believe" this was the truth? (see Carr, 2001c). The work of Burrell and of Farmer asks a similar question, but also echoes the Frankfurt scholars concern that totalizing forms of thinking, such as linear thinking, obscures and marginalizes any "other" and in the process deprives us of reflexive opportunities.

The 'sub-text', that is not so subtly being suggested here, is one that we should give greater priority to examining the philosophy behind the generation of our knowledge and 'truth'. A recently translated fragment of a work written by Benjamin, in 1920-1921, seems to have anticipated our plight. Benjamin (1920-1921/1997c: 276) suggests :

The truth of a given circumstance is a function of the constellation of the true being of all other circumstances. This function is identical with the function of the system. The true being (which as such is naturally unknowable) is part and parcel of the infinite task. However, we have to ask about the medium in which truth and true being are conjoined. What is this neutral medium?

Two things must be overcome:

1. *The false disjunction: knowledge is either in the consciousness of a knowing subject or else in the object (alternatively, identical with it);*
2. *The appearance of the knowing man (for example, Leibniz, Kant).*

The two tasks facing the theory of knowledge are:

1. *The constitution of things in the now of knowability;*
2. *The limitation of knowledge in the symbol.*

Benjamin's words would suggest a discourse, in organization studies and management, of a different character than, with few exceptions, we have seen thus far. Clearly postmodernist approaches to our field have sought to "overcome" the issues raised here by Benjamin. The exploration of art and aesthetics, and alike, affords us an opportunity to more reflexively examine our own field and perhaps take it away from scientism.

References

Adorno, T. (1975). The culture industry reconsidered. *New German Critique*, 6, 12-19.

Adorno, T. (1997). *Aesthetic theory* (R. Hullot-Kentor, Trans.). Minneapolis: University of Minnesota. (Original work published 1970)

Adorno, T. and Horkheimer, M. (1997). *Dialectic of enlightenment* (J. Cumming, Trans.). London: Verso. (Original work published 1944)

Agger, B. (1992). *The discourse of domination: From the Frankfurt School to postmodernism*. Evanston, Illinois: Northwestern University.

Aragon, L. (1971). *Paris peasant* (S. Taylor, Trans.). London: Jonathan Cape. (Original work published 1926)

Benjamin, W. (1997a). Goethe's elective affinities. In M. Bullock, M. and M. Jennings, (Eds.), *Walter Benjamin: Selected writings Volume 1, 1913-1926* (pp. 297-360). Cambridge, MA: Belknap/ Harvard University. (Original work published 1922)

Benjamin, W. (1997b). Surrealism: The Last Snapshot of the European Intelligentsia. In *One-Way Street* (pp. 225-239). London: Verso. (Original work published 1929)

Benjamin, W. (1997c). Theory of knowledge. In M. Bullock, M. and M. Jennings, (Eds.), *Walter Benjamin: Selected writings Volume 1, 1913-1926* (pp. 276-277). Cambridge, MA: Belknap/Harvard University. (Original work written 1920-1921)

Benjamin, W. (1999a). Dream kitsch: Gloss on surrealism. In M. Jennings, H. Eiland & G. Smith, (Eds.), *Walter Benjamin: Selected writings Volume 2, 1927-1934* (pp. 3-5). Cambridge,MA: Belknap/Harvard University. (Original work published 1927)

Benjamin, W. (1999b). Doctrine of the similar. In M. Jennings, H. Eiland & G. Smith, (Eds.), *Walter Benjamin: Selected writings Volume 2, 1927-1934* (pp. 694-698). Cambridge,MA: Belknap/Harvard University. (Original work written January-February 1933)

Benjamin, W. (1999c). On the mimetic faculty. In M. Jennings, H. Eiland & G. Smith, (Eds.), *Walter Benjamin: Selected writings Volume 2, 1927-1934* (pp. 720-727). Cambridge, Massachusetts: Belknap/Harvard University. (Original work written April-September 1933)

Brecht, B. (1957). *Schriften zum theater*. Berlin and Frankfurt:

Suhrkamp.

Breton, A. (1965). Surrealism and painting (Excerpt from Le Surréalisme et la peinture). In P. Waldberg, *Surrealism* (pp. 81-88). London: Thames and Hudson. (Original work published 1927)

Breton, A. (1965). The exquisite corpse (Excerpt from Le Cadavre Exquis: Son Exaltation). In P. Waldberg, *Surrealism* (pp. 93-95). London: Thames and Hudson. (Original work published 1948)

Breton, A. (1969). Manifesto of surrealism (Commonly referred to as the First Manifesto of Surrealism). In *Manifestoes of surrealism*(pp. 1-47) (R. Seaver & H. Lane, Trans.). MI: University of Michigan Ann Arbor. (Original work published 1924)

Breton, A. (1969). Second manifesto of surrealism. In *Manifestoes of surrealism*(pp. 117-194) (R. Seaver & H. Lane, Trans.). MI: University of Michigan Ann Arbor. (Original work published 1930)

Burrell, G. (1997). *Pandemonium: Towards a retro-organization theory*. London: Sage.

Burrell, G. and Morgan, G. (1979). *Sociological paradigms and organizational analysis*. London: Heinemann.

Carr, A. (1996). Putative problematic agency in a postmodern world. *Administrative Theory & Praxis, 18* (1), 79-86 [Later published as Carr, A. (1997). Putative problematic agency in a postmodern world. In H. Miller & C. Fox (Eds.), *Postmodernism, "reality," and public administration: A discourse* (pp. 3-18). VA: Chatelaine].

Carr, A. (1997). Burrell at play: Countering linearity by entering the land of the 'dragons'. *Administrative Theory and Praxis, 19*, 408-413.

Carr, A. (1999). Postmodernism and the turbulence in the social sciences : A brief assessment for the field of business and economics. In D. Kantarelis (Ed.), *Business & Economics for the 21st Century* (Vol. 3, pp. 329-344). Worcester, MA: Business & Economics Society International.

Carr, A. (2000a). The parable of the oarsmen: Adding to Homer in the quest to understand the 'imago' Las Vegas. In J. Biberman & A. Alkhafaji (Eds.), *Business research yearbook: Global business perspectives* (Vol. 7, pp. 697-701). MI: McNaughton & Gunn Inc.

Carr, A. (2000b). Critical theory and the management of change in organizations. In Special Issue on Critical Theory (A. Carr, Ed.). *Journal of Organizational Change Management, 13*, 208-220.

Carr, A. (2001a). Understanding the 'imago' Las Vegas: Taking our lead from Homer's parable of the oarsmen. M@n@gement, 4 (3), 121-140.

Carr, A. (2001b). Organizational and administrative play: The potential of magic realism, surrealism and postmodernist forms of play. In J. Biberman & A. Alkhafaji (Eds.), *Business research yearbook: Global business perspectives* (Vol. 8, pp. 543-547). MI: McNaughton & Gunn.

Carr, A. (2001c). Intellectual IMPOSTURE and French playfulness ("Oh my god they've killed Kenny"): Sokal & Bricmont's attack on French postmodernists. *Administrative Theory & Praxis, 22*, 430-444.

Carr, A. and Zanetti, L. (1998). Surrealism in administrative studies: The fantastic used as a method of elucidation? In D. Farmer (Ed.), *Papers on the art of anti-administration* (pp. 159-196). VA: Chatelaine.

Carr, A. and Zanetti, L. (1999). Metatheorising the dialectics of self and other: The psychodynamics in work organizations. *American Behavioral Scientist*, 43, 324-345.

Carr, A. and Zanetti, L. (2000). The emergence of a surrealist movement and its vital 'estrangement-effect' in organization studies. *Human Relations, 52*, 891-921.

Caws, M. (1997). *The surrealist look: An erotics of encounter.* Cambridge, MA: MIT.

Comte-Sponville, A. (1997). The brute, the sophist, and the aesthete: "Art in the service of illusion". In L Ferry & A. Renaut (Eds.), *Why we are not Nietzscheans* (R. De Loaiza, Trans.) (pp. 21-69). Chicago: University of Chicago. (Original work published 1991)

Cooper, R. and Burrell, G. (1988). Modernism, postmodernism, and organizational analysis: An introduction. *Organization Studies 9* (1), 91-112.

Crimmins, G. (1998). *The republic of dreams: A reverie.* New York: Norton.

Debord, G. (1977). *The society of the spectacle.* Detroit: Clack and Red. (Original work published 1967)

Derrida, J. (1976). *Of grammatology*. Baltimore: John Hopkins.

Farmer, D. (1997a, March). Public administration discourse as (Heraclitean, Derridean) play: Does it pay to play? Paper presented to *The Tenth Symposium On Public Administration Theory*, Richmond, Virginia, March 8-11th 1997 [Later published as Farmer, D. (1997). Public administration discourse as play with a purpose. *Public Voices, 3* (1), 33-51].

Farmer, D. (1997b). Public administration discourse as play with a purpose. *Public Voices, 3* (1), 33-51.

Farmer, D. (1998). Public administration discourse as play with a purpose. In D. Farmer (Ed.), *Papers on the art of anti-administration* (pp. 37-56). VA: Chatelaine.

Freud, S. (1986). *The interpretation of dreams.* Great Britain: Pelican Freud Library, Volume 4. (Original work published 1900)

Fuentes, C. (1998). Introduction. In C. Fuentes & J. Ortega (Eds.), *Latin American stories* (pp. ix-xii). London: Picador.

Gardiner, M. (2000). *Critiques of everyday life.* London: Routledge.

Giroux, H. (1983). *Critical theory and educational practice.* Victoria, Australia: Deakin University.

Gonzalez-Echevarría, R. (1977). *Alejo Carpentíer: The pilgrim at home.* Ithaca: Cornell University.

Handy, C. (1994). *The empty raincoat.* Harmondsworth, England: Penguin.

Held, D. (1995). *Introduction to critical theory: Horkheimer to Habermas.* Cambridge, UK: Polity. (Original work published 1980)

Hohendahl, P. (1995). *Prismatic thought: Theodor W. Adorno.* Lincoln, NE: University of Nebraska.

Honderich, T. (Ed.). (1995). *The Oxford companion to philosophy.* New York: Oxford University.

Homer. *The Odyssey* (E. Rieu, Trans. 1991). Great Britain: Penguin.

Jameson, F. (1991). *Postmodernism, or, the cultural logic of late capitalism.* London: Verso.

Jay, M. (1997a). *Adorno.* Cambridge, MA: Harvard. (Original work published 1984)

Jay, M. (1997b). Mimesis and mimetology: Adorno and Lacoue-Labarthe. In T. Huhn & L. Zuidervaart (Eds.), *The semblance of subjectivity: Essays in Adorno's aesthetic theory* (pp. 29-53). Cambridge, MA: MIT.

Kumar, K. (1995). *From post-industrial to post-modern society.* Oxford, UK: Blackwell.

Kvale, S. (1992). Postmodern psychology. In S. Kvale (Ed.), *Psychology and postmodernism* (pp. 31-57). London: Sage.
Lyotard, J. (1971). *Discours/figure*. Klincksieck: Paris.
Lyotard, J. 1984. *The postmodern condition: A report on knowledge*. Minneapolis: University of Minnesota.
Marcuse, H. (1964). *One dimensional man: Studies in the ideology of advanced industrial society*. London: Routledge & Kegan Paul.
Marcuse, H. (1993). Some remarks on Aragon: Art and politics in the totalitarian era. *Theory, Culture & Society, 10*, 181-195. (Original work written circa unknown)
Marcuse, H. (1998). *Eros and civilization: A philosophical inquiry into Freud*. London: Routledge. (Original work published 1956)
Nicholsen, S. (1997). *Exact imagination, late work on Adorno's aesthetics*. Cambridge, MA: MIT.
Nietzsche, F. (1968). *The will to power* (W. Kaufmann & R. Hollingdale, Trans.). New York: Vintage. (Original work published 1901)
Rasmussen, D. (1996). Critical theory and philosophy. In D. Rasmussen (Ed.), *Handbook of critical theory* (pp. 11-38). Oxford, UK: Blackwell.
Rocco, C. (1994). Between modernity and postmodernity. *Political Theory, 22*, 71-97.
Rochlitz, R. (1996). *The disenchantment of art: The philosophy of Walter Benjamin* (J. Todd, Trans.). New York: Guilford. (Original work published 1992)
Rosenau, P. (1992). *Post-modernism and the social sciences: Insights, inroads, and intrusions*. Princeton, NJ: Princeton University.
Sarup, M. (1993). *An introduction guide to post-structuralism and postmodernism* (2nd ed.). Athens, GA: University of Georgia.
Sawin, M. (1995). *Surrealism in exile and the beginning of the New York School*. Cambridge, MA: MIT.
Spector, J. (1997). *Surrealist art and writing 1919/39: The gold of time*. Cambridge, NY: University of Cambridge.
Waldberg, P. (1997). *Surrealism*. London: Thames and Hudson. (Original work published 1965)
Wiggershaus, R. (1994). *The Frankfurt School* (M. Robertson, Trans.). Cambridge, MA: MIT.
Winnicott, D. (1971a). *Playing and reality*. New York: Basic Books.

Winnicott, D. (1971b). Transitional objects and transitional phenomena. In D. Winnicott, *Playing and reality* (pp. 1-25). New York: Basic Books.

Winnicott, D. (1971c). Playing: A theoretical statement. In D. Winnicott, *Playing and reality* (pp. 38-52). New York: Basic Books.

Winnicott, D. (1971d). The location of cultural experience. In D. Winnicott, *Playing and reality* (pp. 95-103). New York: Basic Books.

Winnicott, D. (1971e). The place where we live. In D. Winnicott, *Playing and reality* (pp. 104-110). New York: Basic Books.

Wolin, R. (1997). Benjamin, Adorno, surrealism. In T. Huhn & L. Zuidervaart (Eds.), *The semblance of subjectivity: Essays in Adorno's aesthetic theory* (pp. 93-122). Cambridge, MA: MIT

Appendix A: Similarity of Surrealism and Postmodernism
(Carr, 1999, p. 339)

SURREALISM	*POSTMODERNISM(/POSTSTRUCTURALISM)* **Management/Org Studies discourse**
GENERAL ORIENTATION	
To transcend rationality, linear thinking and the control and presence of the "author". Seeking what might be called 'the language of the soul', that is, the expression — stripped of all logical device — of the profound 'me' in its nakedness" (Waldberg 1965/1997, p. 13). Some surrealists such as Desmond Morris (1987) did not believe their work was part of revealing some form of essentialism of being, but simply it was "visual play".	Central and recurrent themes of postmodernism are that "*it's all in the text*" and the importance of *the death-of-the-subject*. Postmodernists embrace the early poststructuralist view that 'truth' is merely a construction of language. Moreover, the human as a subject is likewise simply part of that text, nothing more than a transient epiphenomenon of a specific and local cultural discourse.
'TECHNIQUES' (Not a strict correspondence but overlapping affinity)	
Exquisite Corpse - a stringing together of arbitrary chosen phrases by different poets unaware of what preceded or followed.	**Intertwining of form and content** - formatting 'text' in a way which tries to escape linearity and conventional logic eg. in Burrell's (1997) book "Pandemonium" page numbering is on the side of the page, often flanked by an arrow to give the reader an indication of where to read next. There is a "dual carriageway in which text across the top half of the page moving from left to right 'meets' text moving from right to left across the bottom half of the page. Pages have a central reservation which it is always dangerous to cross" (p. 2). Free association is encouraged by this technique.
Automatic writing - writing quickly without control, self-censorship, or thought for the outcome in terms of literary merit, making free associations as they seem to flow.	**Playfulness and the play of irony** - engaging questions such as — "what if it wasn't like this but the opposite?" It is through the *clash-of-opposites* that we may transcend the logic and rationality of the day. In the example of Burrell's medieval tale of Pandemonium, a historical setting full of despair, images of death and decay is designed to shock our sensibilities. **Clash-of-opposites** - overturning an implied hierarchy and 'reading' of a text by disturbing the conventional associations - see deconstruction and playfulness.
'Dreams' or inducing a dream-like state to give the unconscious unimpeded passage.	
Metaphoricality - exquisite corpse could be used in drawing and suggested it was "an infallible way of holding the critical intellect in abeyance, and of fully liberating the mind's *metaphorical activity*" (Breton 1948/1965, p. 95).	**Metaphoricality** - the use of metaphors not just to capture a general idea but to be used as a tool to help us see that which is hidden or obscured from our everyday vision and consciousness.
(The Visual arts) Questioned the familiar identity of objects by faithfully reproducing them on canvas or in spaces but placing them in unfamiliar settings and using such unfamiliar associations to produce a kind of poetic strangeness. The shock of juxtaposing objects in unfamiliar association elicited unforeseen affinities between objects and, perhaps, unexpected emotion and sensations in the observer. A similar philosophy was applied in the technique of **Collage** - reassemble objects on a canvas without concern for how they might be arranged and juxtaposed.	**Deconstruction** - an introspective activity that seeks to unsettle the taken for granted meaning and assumptions of a text by using the text against itself e.g., by *erasing* one word/concept, and substituting its 'opposite' also by scanning the text for contradictions and disruptions in the words, expressions, and ideas that are used and by so doing, putatively, exposing a text's logocentrism.
Other techniques which are variations of those listed above: Automatic drawing and painting, Decalcomania and **Frottage.**	

Notes

[1] It is noteworthy that very few commentators on Adorno's *Aesthetic Theory* have attempted to come to terms with his concept of enigma, and, indeed, how it is related to mimesis. Nicholsen is an exception and

an exception well worth reading for the profound incite she brings to the work of Adorno. Nicholsen does not, however, pursue the logical conclusion of projecting Adorno's argument further. If mimesis is enactment behavior in which self seeks assimilation to other, then enigma would seem to represent an other to other. Thinking about this more laterally, the dialectical assimilation of self to other and other to self (see Carr & Zanetti, 1999) would in the same process appear to 'create', as an artifact of that process, an other that remained unassimilated—unassimilated as it represented a quality, or in Nicholsen's words "being nonconceptual".

[2] It could be said that Adorno was hesitant toward embracing the work of the surrealists—a conclusion reached by Wolin (1997) with which I concur. Adorno seemed to think surrealists fetishize certain object and representations, producing a form of reification. The production of such images was carried out with little awareness of the mediated nature of their production. The whole work, in his view, is programmatic and becomes one imbued with rationality with the sole intention to shock and provoke. The problem I see in this position is that Adorno has failed to distinguish between the different 'techniques' used by the surrealists and he appears less than sensitive to the different form that surrealism may have to take in different arts. This said, Adorno was sympathetic to montage and in his last major work, *Aesthetic Theory* (1970/1997), surprisingly praised the surrealists for the ability to produce the "shock effect" and in so doing defetishize and help disarm everyday rationality (see also commentaries by Agger, 1992: 228; Held, 1980/1995: 104-105; Hohendahl, 1995: 211; Jay, 1984/1997a: 129-131).

[3] The word exaggerated is used here as I am very mindful of the way in which the Frankfurt scholars saw the critical function of art and aesthetics being over-powered. Gardiner (2000) reads this situation similarly when he says:

In the perspective of Adorno et al., techniques of social control had become perfected to such an extent, and 'false consciousness' so pervasive, that moments of no-alienated or emancipated experience could only be glimpsed furtively in the most avant-garde of artworks and forms of theoretical production, in aesthetics and intellectual experiences which, by virtue of their very complexity and symbolic opacity, resisted absorption into what they termed the 'culture industry' (p. 15).

The dynamics of the culture industry are discussed in the next section of this paper.

[4] See Carr and Zanetti (1998, 2000) for a much larger discussion of surrealism and the connection with the work of the critical theorists Adorno, Benjamin and Marcuse, and, also, the parallels with aspects of the work of post modernists/post structuralists.

[5] Hegel argued that dialectical thought begins with a "thesis", any definable reality that is the starting point from which all further de-

velopment proceeds. As reflection progresses, this thesis is seen to encompass its opposite, or "antithesis", *as part of its very definition.* The triadic structure of Hegelian thought is not simply a series of building blocks. Each triad represents a process wherein the synthesis absorbs and completes the two prior terms, following which the entire triad is absorbed into the next higher process. Hegel himself preferred to refer to the dialectic as a system of negations, rather than triads. His purpose was to overcome the static nature of traditional philosophy and capture the dynamics of reflective thought. The essence of the dialectic is the ability to see wholes and the conflict of parts simultaneously.

[6] Of course the surrealists, like the Dadaist movement, often satirized and mocked bourgeois society, but such satire and mocking was reliant upon the extent to which the irony and juxtaposition could continue to create this unease and not 'simply' be taken as an aesthetic presentation and get otherwise absorbed into a world of advertising and kitsch. Indeed, in the case of Dada, as one of its leaders, Richard Huelsenbeck claimed: "The Dadaist considers it necessary to come out against art (painting, sculpture, culture, spirit, athletic club) because he has seen through its fraud as a moral safety valve" (Cited in Gardiner, 2000: 29). It was the repressive and ideological content carried in art that Dadaists found so objectionable. The Dadaist endeavored to escape anything that was traditional or common sense by engaging the spontaneous and the by-chance. Some of the 'techniques' for exploring the spontaneous and by-chance were to find their way into that later movement called "surrealism". Of course, the spontaneity and by-chance as an avenue to the repressed had also being championed by Freud in his notion of free association and Jung and his concept of synchronicity. The anarchistic and provocative 'stunts', and the nihilistic orientation, of the Dadaist were, however, not the path of the surrealist. Although originally followers of Dada, the founding surrealists sought a "radical renewal of means; to pursue the same ends [as Dada], but by markedly different paths" (Breton - cited in Gardiner, 2000: 33). The path of the surrealist was more programmatic, aimed at the dawn of an intellectual revolution and not merely at protest, non-conformity, stunts, irrationality for its own sake and acts of destructive agitation.

[7] For some, the position that these scholars are expressing on art and its function could be seen as elitist, simply just one point of view, a personal preference, or merely an expression of taste. I think the key point here is, however, that Adorno and Horkheimer have identified that art appeared to have a critical function which, as will be noted in this next section, has been surrendered or lost in the context of the rise of a culture industry. It is the analysis of this loss that is the focus and as such is beyond the realm of simply a matter of taste [see also Jameson (1991: 298-289) for a parallel argument on postmodernism].

The issue of kitsch was a significant matter for some scholars of the Frankfurt School. Adorno and Benjamin were very careful in their interpretation of kitsch. Adorno (1970/1997) argued:

Kitsch is not, as those believers in erudite culture would like to imagine the mere refuse of art, originating in disloyal accommodation to the enemy; rather it lurks in art, awaiting ever recurring opportunities to spring forth. Although kitsch escapes, implike, from even a historical definition, one of its most tenacious characteristics is the prevarication of feelings, fictional feelings in which no one is actually participating, and thus the neutralization (italics added) of these feelings. Kitsch parodies catharsis. Ambitious art, however, produces the same fiction of feelings; indeed, this was essential to it: The documentation of actually existing feelings, the recapitulation of psychical raw material, is foreign to it. It is in vain to try to draw the boundaries abstractly between aesthetic fiction and kitsch's emotional plunder. It is poison admixed to all art; excising it is today one of art's despairing efforts (p. 239).

Benjamin (1927/1999a), in the context of discussing surrealism, refers to kitsch in the following manner:

Picture puzzles, as schemata of the dreamwork, were long ago discovered by psychoanalysis. The Surrealists, with a similar conviction, are less on the trail of the psyche than on the track of things. They seek the totemic tree of objects within the thicket of primal history. The very last, the topmost face of the totem pole, is that of kitsch. It is the last mask of the banal, the one with which we adorn ourselves, in dream and conversation, so as to take in the energies of an outlived world of things.

What we used to call art begins at a distance of two meters from the body. But now, in kitsch, the world of things advances on the human being; it yields to his uncertain grasp and ultimately fashions its figures in his interior. The new man bears within himself the very quintessence of the old forms, and what evolves in the confrontation with a particular milieu from the second half of the nineteenth century—in the dreams, as well as the words and images, of certain artists—is a creature who deserves the name of "furnished man" (pp. 4-5).

[8] I have placed Horkheimer in brackets as much of this chapter of the book, including the first draft, was clearly written by Adorno (see Wiggershaus, 1994: 323). Also much of the line of argument emerges from Adorno's earlier work in which he was the single author and which I cite in this section of the paper.
[9] The term "Enlightenment" is used frequently in this paper and has an assumed philosophical meaning. For those unfamiliar with the philosophy of enlightenment, the doctrines of Enlightenment include: reason is crucial to the capacity to act; humans are by nature rational and good; individuals and humanity as a whole can progress to perfection; all persons are created equal and should be accorded equality

before the law and individual liberty; tolerance is to be afforded to all groups in society; beliefs are accepted only on the basis of reason (note: often the Age of Enlightenment is called the Age of Reason); rationality is the universal binding force that transcends differences in culture and creed and as such devalues customs and local practices to the extent that they maybe historically based rather than the exercise of reason; the non-rational is to take a back seat to the rational, thus education is to be viewed as imparting knowledge rather than developing feeling, emotions, and art as the product of good taste rather than genius (see Honderich, 1995: 236-237).

[10] Adorno and Horkheimer often used the terms *culture* and *art* interchangeably but in other instances were more disciplined and used culture as a more generic term that includes art, music, film etc. This is an important point as in their chapter on the culture industry when they refer to art they mean the arts more generally as in culture, yet they also single out the world of art, as in painting, as an example.

[11] In using the term "capitalism", I am prompted to comment that readers of *Dialectic of Enlightenment* need to be aware that some terms were changed from the mimeographed edition of 1944. Euphemisms were inserted such that: capitalism became "existing conditions"; capital became "economic systems"; capitalist bloodsuckers was changed to "knights of industry"; class society became "domination" or "order"; and, ruling class became "rulers" (see Wiggershaus, 1994: 410). There were other small changes to phrases and certain phrases that were omitted, in acts of self censorship, in the interests of maintaining the goodwill and support of the American authorities. The Institute for Social Research, in Germany, that was the home of the Frankfurt School scholars was closed in 1933, under the Nazi regime, for tendencies deemed hostile to the State. The Institute moved its home, temporarily, to Geneva and then to New York, becoming affiliated with Columbia University. The Institute did not return to Frankfurt until 1949.

[12] Adorno and Horkheimer used the now familiar tale by Homer of Odysseus to particularly highlight the dynamics of such a prolongation of work. For Adorno and Horkheimer the reconciliation of the apparent antagonism between work and pleasure, that appears in the tale, is attempted in the modern bourgeois in the same way, i.e., in the contemplation of art. The ancient tale is viewed by them as a parable for more recent times. Adorno and Horkheimer explain this 'lesson' and simultaneously provide a restatement of Hegel's master-servant parable:

Whoever would survive must not hear the temptation of that which is unrepeatable, and he is able to survive only by being unable to hear it. Society has always made provision for that. The laborers must be fresh and concentrate as they look ahead, and must ignore whatever lies to one side. They must doggedly sublimate in additional effort the drive that impels diversion. And so they become practical. – The other possibility Odysseus, the seigneur who allows the others to labor for themselves, reserves to himself... They (the oarsmen) reproduce the oppressor's life together with their own, and the oppressor is no longer able to escape his social role. The bonds with which he has irremediably tied himself to practice, also keep Sirens away from practice: their temptation is neutralized and becomes a mere object of contemplation—becomes art... Thus the enjoyment of art and manual labor break apart as the world of prehistory is left behind. The epic already contains the appropriate theory. The cultural material is in exact correlation to work done according to command; and both are grounded in the inescapable compulsion to social domination of nature.

Measures such as those taken on Odysseus' ship in regard to the Sirens form presentiment allegory of the dialectic of enlightenment. Just as the capacity of representation is the measure of domination, and domination is the most powerful thing that can be represented in most performances, so the capacity of representation is the vehicle of progress and regression at one and the same time (Adorno & Horkheimer, 1944/1997: 34-35).

For a larger discussion of the manner in which the reconciliation of the apparent antagonism between work and pleasure has modern significance, see Carr's paper "Understanding the 'imago' Las Vegas: Taking our lead from Homer's parable of the oarsmen" (2001a).

[13] Further to the previous footnote, this view has much in common and, in some senses, anticipated some of the work of Guy-Ernest Debord and his notion of "Spectacle" (1967/1977). Debord described how, through capitalist rationalization, the individual had become alienated in a world of circulating images. Life was a spectacle to be watched from a distance rather than something the individual was an active participant and over which s/he had some sovereignty.

[14] For more discussion of this argument see Carr (1997), also Carr and Zanetti (1998, 2000).

[15] In noting the nihilism of both surrealists and postmodernists it is not the intention to infer that, philosophically, such a position can be held as some kind of 'ideal-type'. In the case of postmodernists, I have specifically challenged they fit into such a black and white labelling system, for they do hold a value position that focuses and privileges the neglected, the silent, the hidden and gives primacy to the 'reader' over the 'author' (see Carr, 1996).

Chapter 2
Organizational Performance: A View from the Arts

Ceri Watkins & Ian W. King

Organizational Performance: A View from the Arts

In the early part of the 20th century a great upheaval took place in many fields of human endeavour, with qualities, values, or techniques that had been relied on in previous centuries to provide meaning, no longer retaining their efficacy. Traditional frames of reference such as perspective in painting, Euclidian geometry, tonality in music, temporal sequence in narrative, unvarying temporal and spatial reference frames in physics, were challenged and overthrown by new forms of understanding.

We intend to suggest that this tidal wave of change has passed over most of our current understanding of organizational performance, leaving it in a stagnated pool of passé thinking. This paper proposes that organizations are still attempting to apprehend and represent the world utilizing strategies and understandings that were predominant in the early part of the 20th century and thus exerted a massive influence during the infancy of management thinking. Influences, which despite their undoubted success in the past, may no longer be as appropriate for the current organizational environment. It is intended to demonstrate how thinking in other fields have embraced new values and understandings, and have thus moved on from these outmoded forms of thought, in attempts to develop more apposite ways of engaging with the world.

To do this we draw upon Stephen Kern's idea of 'conceptual distance', and Bakhtin's similar notion of 'ideological adequation' to demonstrate the values underpinning the thinking in some of these areas, and to show that they are quite different from those of most organizational thought. Kern (1983: 7) suggests that "there is greater conceptual distance between the thinking of an architect and that of a philosopher on a given subject than there is between the thinking of two philosophers, and I assume that any generalizations about the thinking of an age is the more persuasive the greater conceptual distance between the sources on which it is based". Thus considering thinking that is apparently, conceptually separated from each other, may allow us to identify underpinning values, that act as an aid to successful understanding in our current environment. To do this we intend to utilise the fields of painting and literary narrative, showing how their understandings have radically changed from those still in use in organizations. Drawing on this we then go on to suggest that organizations may be able to exploit this body of knowledge in order to further its own understanding.

Stagnation

The last forty years or so of Management literature demonstrates, a desire, or evidence of, a striving toward increasingly effective performance in organizations. Despite this attention it might be claimed that the whole notion of what is performance remains elusive, with few definitions which adequately encompass the character of performance in organizations. A closer examination of the management literature suggests that much of what is considered organizational performance, would be much better viewed as a feature of the measurement technique selected, and as such is better seen as part of a self-referential discourse that acts to define the object of study. A discourse, which it can be clearly seen it is anchored in a mode of perception dominant from the Renaissance until the early 1900s.

This discourse is about providing evidence of, or prescriptions for, or remedies to, organizational action that supposedly, no, that are themselves convinced, will undoubtedly lead to improved, superior, optimal, fantastic (etc.) outcomes. Looming large within this diatribe lie rules and regulations that specify consistent levels of action. Rules that regulate a constancy that provides stakeholders with feelings of confidence in the quality of the organization and the service or goods, that they are producing, sampling or seeking to purchase. We can find evidence of the role of rules and regulations ranging from safety to health and from quality to service.

These rules, it might be argued, are manifestations of the desire by the managements of organizations to seemingly impose an appearance of 'seamlessness'. Thus performance in organizations becomes perceived as a seamless progression of the quantitative, often financial, measures that the various prescriptions for successful performance have mandated as the accepted symbols, or sign posts, of that performance. For management, the achievement of this reduction, where all the steps naturally follow on, prevents personnel from considering alternative, perhaps contradictory or deviating, courses of action, and thus the organization can guarantee, what they perceive as, optimal standards and quality. This is the narrative, a story of striving for efficiency and excellence, which organizations, the public and so many academics find irresistibly seductive. It is to the source of this seduction that we now turn.

The Seductiveness of an Easy Story

For us, Gombrich (1982) encapsulates the reason for this situation when he describes how a musician reads and understands a musical score with surprising ease and at amazing speed:

does he not have to take in information at an uncanny rate? Certainly the feat is admirable, but it is only possible because the notes of the score... are not unconnected signs. Music is an art that follows certain laws or rules, which enable the musician to scan the score with certain expectations. Though he cannot know what to expect in the next bar, he knows at least that many possibilities are ruled out. Indeed if any of those occurred he would probably disregarded it as a misprint. In reading a familiar language of course, we proceed a similar way, looking ahead for cues to conform to our expectations and filling in the remainder more or less from experience ... assumptions of this kind are so ingrained in us that it needs quite a jolt to prevent our interpretation from running along these convenient grooves (p. 154).

It is this ease, the seductiveness of a clear path to follow, that organizations and their stakeholders appear to crave, to be able to read organizational performance, quickly and easily, allowing judgements to be made, decisions actioned, and to thus continue the onward march to success. It is a craving firmly anchored in the Western tradition of thought since the Renaissance, and manifest in its discourse obsessed with "power and knowledge, its constraint of language to primarily symbolic function, its ethic of winning, its categorical and dualistic modes of definition, its belief in the quantitative and objective, its linear time and individual subject, and above all its common media of exchange (time, space, money) which guarantee certain political and social systems" (Ermarth, 1992: 7).

To satisfy this craving for success and ease of understanding, has required the development of '*rules to follow*', that through defining what is acceptable inform our expectations, and allow us to predetermine the range of potential possibilities, discarding in advance much of '*organizational action*', and like our musician earlier disregarding anything that does not conform to our schema as a '*misprint*' or irrelevant. The essence of utilizing a set of rules is that it narrows the area for consideration, eliminates and simplifies. Here it is suggested that the modernist rule based understanding of organizations is so embedded in management culture, that its ingrained assumptions are very rarely recognized let alone considered. Thus the '*reading*' of organizational performance within these frameworks requires the (often unaware) dismissal, of organizational actions and characteristics that do not conform, as '*misprints*' or irrelevancies. However it may be that what these rules encourage to be, or insist are, dismissed is far from irrelevant, and may even be vital, to understanding and survival for organizations into the 21st-century.

This may even help explain the enormous success of the many prescriptions for outstanding organizational performance based on simple rules that ease understanding. Whether it is Peters and Waterman's (1982) rules for excellence, the mantra of *Business Process Reengineering* (Hammer, 1990), or the promises of management in a minute . Furthermore it may intimate the source of many management difficulties, and provide pointers to explain the sometimes spectacular demise of Peters and Waterman's 'excellent companies' or the devastation caused by much *Business Process Reengineering*.

Furthermore the search for sets of rules, to solve the riddle of how to produce '*outstanding performance*' dominates the performance literature. Tsoukas (1995: 5) highlights how management thinking is dominated by "search for the regularities exhibited by social systems, [to] establish their validity and codify them in the form of rules (that is, 'if, then' statements) which managers would then be able to put into practice with confidence". A position clearly established by March and Sutton for the field of research into organizational performance, who demonstrated that "most studies of organizational performance define performance as a dependent variable and seek to identify variables that produce variations in performance" (March & Sutton, 199: 698), and the continuing ubiquity of which, we invite the reader to confirm for themselves, by simply browsing a few recent issues of highly regarded journals such as the *Strategic Management Journal*, the *Academy of Management Journal* or the *Administrative Science Quarterly*. This body of literature amounts to a search for the if/then rules that will hopefully allow the improvement of performance. It implies that once the correct relationships are established, then simply by following the requisite prescriptions, such as for example amending board member diversity (Siciliano, 1996) or market and quality orientation (Sussan & Johnson, 1997), it will enable the holy grail of improved performance to be achieved.

Yet, despite the continued ascendancy of this type of approach it is not without its critics, we next examine some manifestations of disquiet with the dominance of rules and prescription, before going on to illustrate how both narrative and painting have faced similar misgivings with these forms of representation and understanding, and have thus attempted to overcome their comparable dilemmas.

Organizational Disquiet

Evidence of dissatisfaction with the current situation in organizations could be heard in a recent edition of the BBC radio programme *Analysis,* entitled *Rough Counting*, which was broadcast in November 1999 (Hassler, 1999). A number of leading academics, industrialists, consultants and government appointed heads of regulatory bodies, discussed the increasing trend within organizations to become *rule-governed.* In essence the programme revealed, the increasing unease of all parties, with organization's penchant for turning to rules, and away from their own abilities of '*competence*'. They seem to be searching out every opportunity to turn toward government for further guidance, and in particular rules to prescribe their behavior. It is almost tantamount to a fear of operating in a 'space without rules', an unwillingness to engage with a depth of possibilities. Time and time again the former heads of the regulatory bodies lamented the inability of a wide variety of organizations to do more than adhere to these rules!

As Colette Bowe (Executive Chairperson of Save & Prosper, and former head of the Personal Investment Authority) explained, some organization's even requested more rules.

BOWE: actually we would like some prescription please. Because if we are going to get into serious trouble as many firms in this industry have done, if we are going to be fined, because of things like the practices of our sales force, we need to know precisely what it is, you regulators who have these draconian powers, are expecting us to do. Now I always very much regretted that, when I was a regulator, I used to constantly say to people don't keep asking us for rules, don't keep asking us for rules, you know what the fundamental duty is, do it. But this industry has said, we would like prescription please, we want to be sure. It requires I think, enormous confidence in your own professionalism to be able to say, thanks fine, I know what it means to know my customers, leave it to me to work out what that means.

A point further emphasized by Clare Spottiswoode, (member of the management team of PA Consulting, London and former Regulator of the Gas Industry) and Peter Miller (Professor of Accounting, London School of Economics)

SPOTTISWOODE: You can't run a company with a whole set of rules, what you have to do is say, what are we trying to achieve her

MILLER: Without doubt one of my favorite phrases is 'What is counted, counts', and as soon as we start counting something we tend to become fixed on it.

Even the leaders of professions that are built around control and prescription find organization's current fixation on rules disturbing. Mike Jeans (President of CIMA) berates business's dependence on "successive waves of laws and rules" (Times, 2001: 15), suggesting that this is problematic, in that these systems of control, and the mindsets that go with it, are "unlikely to build a future; rather, it preserves the past and, perhaps, the present" (*ibid.*). He identifies that organizations "are seeking ways of releasing organizational potential through flexibility, empowerment, valuing diversity, working as teams, challenging the status quo, etc" (ibid) and as such realize conventions based on rules and control are inhibitive and obsolete, and need to be '*blown up*'.

Making a similar point on the problematic nature of rule based conceptions of performance, Dobson (1999) argues that attempts at developing rule based systems of performing (in this case through rules of business ethics) is futile. That any attempts to do so flounder when confronted with the difficulties in operating in a business reality that is '*complex, multifarious, and ephemeral*' and thus essentially '*chaotic and unpredictable*'.

It is to two different fields of understanding, art and literature, that have also faced the difficulties inherent in the fixed nature of a rules informed approach to apprehending the world, to which we turn to further explore this phenomenon.

Rules and Perspective in Painting

Art, and in particular painting, provides for us evidence for our argument. For painting too was stifled in the past by its heavy reliance on rules. The pre-occupation of artists for these rules revealed for many of them the limitations of their art and yet still they wished to develop its potential—it is with this experience in mind we seek to reveal how as students of management and organizations, we might gain from their trials and tribulations. In contrast to the earlier discussion of organizations, painting has not shown the same degree of fear of rules, and the possibilities and problems it may present, despite arguably parallel historical precedents.

However, for over four centuries painting was also to a great degree dominated by the rigid rules and lines of perspective, as expounded in Alberti's defining text of 1435, *De Pictura*, and which came to define the rules for determining acceptable verisimilitude. He likened a painted picture to an open window, thus a picture, in his view, should be made to seem as if it were a pane of transparent glass through which we look into an imaginary space extending into depth. This along with parallel developments in the Flemish schools, expounded by amongst others Jan Van Eyck, directed the future of the painting clearly down the rigid path of rule-laden perspective.

The rules of modern representation and scale preclude the portrayal of individuals inside buildings, or out of scale, to promote recognition and understanding prevalent before the reign of perspective . All that is not encapsulated by the perspective delineated segment of reality is obscured and marginalized. As Stella proposes, "something as simple as a mobile viewpoint seems to be an anathema. We are so conditioned by the window of perspective that we stand motionless in front of it, waiting for painting to organise itself according to our acquired habits" (Stella, 1986: 51). The space in painting became available to eyesight alone; intuition or insight, to apprehend understanding became redundant. This can be illustrated if we examine Caneletto's picture below (Figure 1). Here we can infer that the building and walls contain and hide individuals within, and behind, importance or allegory play no role in their portrayal, they are inviolably circumscribed by line and scale.

Consequently we sense that artists around this time were seeking to persuade observers and other painters of their skill in depicting the 'real'. The absence in earlier paintings, of perspective, tended to leave the observer with the impression that the image was flat. The image lacked realism. With the initial introduction of perspective, the depth and richness of object becomes more apparent, more alive—it almost reaches out to the viewer "[A] single network of lines can create an effect of depth that implies that the negation, or—as the phenomenonologists would put it—the neantization, of the plane onto which it is projected, to the gain of the image inscribed there" (Damisch, 1994: 11). Here the image almost engages the viewer and persuades them of its realism. With this tech-

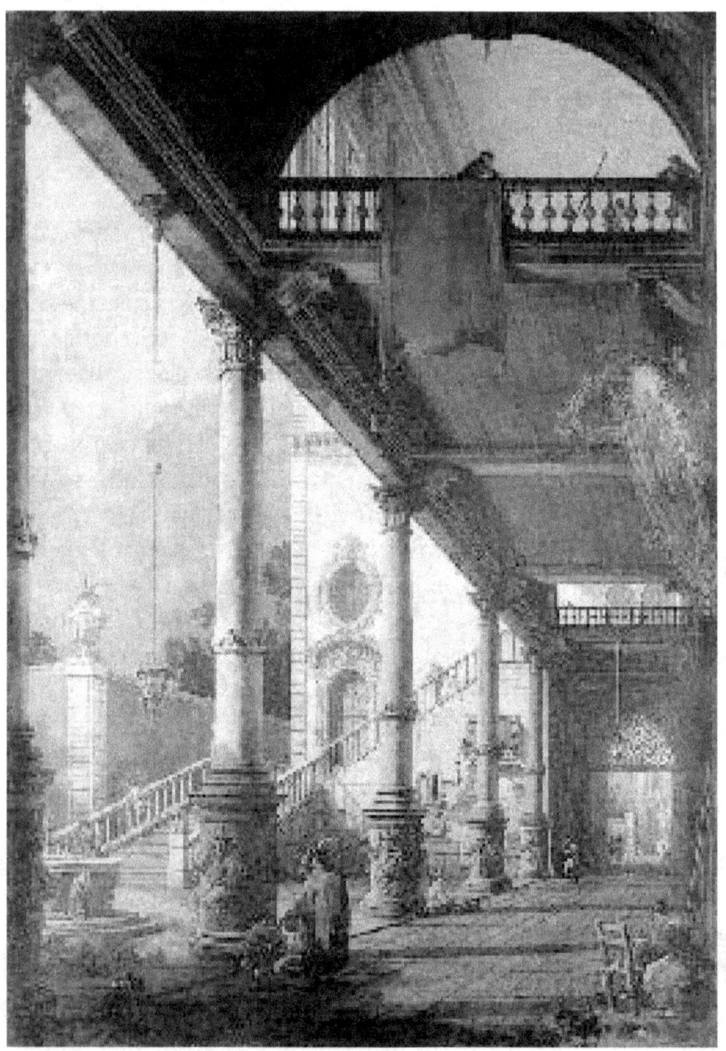

Figure 1

nique, and for the viewer to grasp meaning and generate understanding from a painting requires only knowledge and application of the rules of perspective . It enabled a separation of not only the artist from the reality they are attempting to depict, but a separation of the viewer, spatially, temporally and culturally from that which they are trying to understand. The separation, despite requiring rules if understanding is to be realized, provides for a smoother and less taxing mode of interpretation. The seductiveness of this approach which allowed 'an easy form of interpretation', where only a knowledge and application of a set of universally appropriate rules, was necessary, encouraged what could be considered a form of 'collusion' between both artist and viewer. It led to the atrophy of the more strenuous requirements for contextual understanding and informed interpretation. Representations informed by the rules of perspective became considered as a 'true depiction' for most of society, the idealization and simplification inherent in this practise, unrecognized or conveniently forgotten.

Such was the seductiveness of this form of persuasion it soon became codified into a set of rules for the achievement of persuasive perspective, rules that became ossified into an array of almost unchallengeable prescriptions for artists, if they wanted to participate in what was considered by many the only acceptable realist representation. Thus painting itself became caught up in one set of rules, a situation that may be considered analogous to the illustration we gleaned from the BBC *Rough Counting* radio programme of management's craving for rules to follow, and the dominance of the performance literature by a search for the rules that produce effective performance.

The Perspectival Understanding of Management

It has been argued that the emergence of perspective into Western consciousness during the 14th century is one of the defining moments in the birth of what has become known as modernism . The advent of the lens of perspective, brought to the world a sense of space, and spatiality. Human vision became conditioned to perceive space, and in particular those features which lie within this space, in a quite different way. As Ivins explains, methods of perspectival pictorial representation have become pervasive as they:

have provided symbols, repeatable in invariant form, for representation of visual awareness, and a grammar of perspective which made it possible to establish logical relations not only within the system of symbols but between that system and the forms and locations of the objects that it symbolizes (pp. 12-13).

This abstraction enabled a depiction of space as being measurable, and as such reducible, to the measurements involved. Thus the separation of humanity from the object of perception, along with the depiction of that object using the symbolic forms of perspective, has fuelled a drive "to measure everything measurable and to make what is not measurable capable of being measured" (Palmer, 1977: 22). Such was the strength of this move toward measurement, that those aspects which could not be measured, for example intuition, magic and the occult, are pushed aside or consigned to some form stigmatised category (i.e. witchcraft, superstition, guesswork). Thus, this spatialization, and the agenda to make everything visualizable, and therefore measurable has had consequences beyond that of pictorial representation . As Damisch (1994: 28) suggests, perspective can be considered "as something that is productive of effects, in so far as its capacity, its power to inform extends well beyond the limits of the era in which it was born." He elaborates that "[W]ithout any doubt, our period is ... massively 'informed' by the perspective paradigm".

This perspectival understanding, emphasizes the separation of object from observer and attempts the division of the separated object into measurable terms. Which has lead to the eclipse and marginalization of phenomenon that cannot be easily spatially depicted and reliably measured. For art the lines of perspective, define and illuminate part of a scene, bring into scrutiny certain aspects of the whole, aspects that are ascribed an unwarranted primacy. Yet for all that it illuminates, it also casts shadows. Perspective obscures, hides behind lines/corners, diminishes and minimizes much of the totality it attempts to represent. Rigid rules prescribe what can and cannot be seen, what to disregard as irrelevant, size and scale are incontestably linked to the measures of space and distanciation employed. It dictates how reality may be depicted, and which part of that reality is therefore given legitimacy. The unbearable constraints of these rules are frequently illustrated using the famous Durer woodcut (Figure 2), "in effect, it shows an artist caught up in a veritable pillory as he draws the contours of a (nude) model in front of him, gazing at her through a transparent, squared screen, his eye immobile at the tip of a stiletto" (Damisch, 1994: 36). It shows how the representation is produced utilizing the rules of perspective, which are physically manifest in the mechanical devices employed.

As intimated earlier, management as a discipline emerged from these same insights, where all behaviors could be reduced to measurement and evaluation. It was the enthusiasm of F. W. Taylor (amongst others) and his methods—which were at least popular with managements—that drove its development down the road of striving to place all of its activities into classifiable categories and controllable variables. We see it all around us in organizations, their presence, their past and their future. Management and organizations are dominated, and assessed by, scientific rules and procedures. Thus just as with Durer's artist, who's representation is constricted by the rules and technology of perspective, so to is manage-

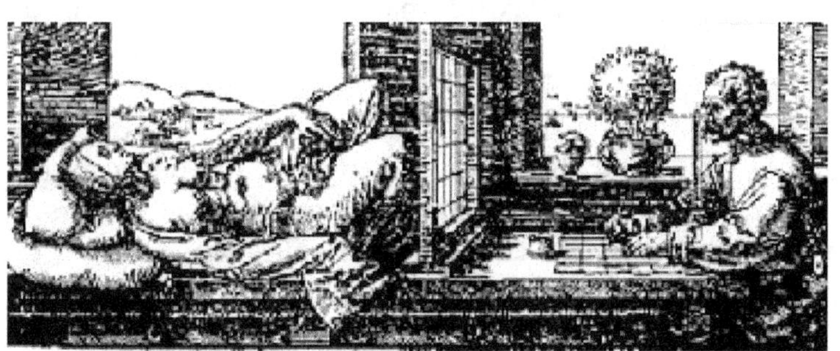

Figure 2

ment's understanding, through its perspectival informed, modernist technologies, of rationality and measurement. As Peter Miller (Professor of Accounting from the London School of Economics) said in the BBC radio programme introduced above:

Without doubt one of my favorite phrases is 'What is counted counts', as soon as we start counting something we tend to become fixed on it.

Literary Conventions

Here we explore how in the field of literature similar conventions, in the form of the realist novel, dominated literature's approach to representing reality, before it underwent a major discursive shift during the intellectual upheaval of the early twentieth century.

Prior to this discursive shift, novelistic conventions were dominated by aesthetic canon that supported and were supported by, the principal cultural values elaborated earlier. The primary assumption of novelistic intent was to "mirror reality, especially to reflect the unity and integrity of the world" (Vargish & Mook, 1998: 38), in an almost exact parallel to the role of perspective in painting. For readers of these novels it was the role of the narrator to stand at the single point perspective, and 'tell it as it is/ was. Thus just as viewers of paintings 'colluded' with the artist so a "fundamental understanding between the reader and author was sustained: the narrator narrates the real world, an 'objective' world, that exists independent of the narrator's perception, whether that world be natural, social or psychological" (Vargish & Mook, 1998: 39).

Elizabeth Ermarth (1983) elegantly and effectively argues, that a similar act of collusion occurs between this narrator (whether explicit or implicit) and the readers, in a commonality with that of painter and viewer. Thus the narrator acts in, and or, evokes a world, underpinned by the same values as those of perspectival representation. The dominance and ubiquity of the realist novel, along with the fame and familiarity of its great protagonists, such as Bronte, Dickens, Eliot, Tolstoy, Twain and Flaubert, suggests very little is needed in the way of further exemplification. So, for a suitably brief exposition, it is to one of these great exponents that we turn. Dickens, in his writing "however different [his] moods, what informs his evocations is always an unabating interest in this world, and in this society as a thing real and, as to its reality, wholly unproblematic" (Stern, 1973: 5). Thus in for example *Little Dorrit* "the various parallels of plot, scene, and image conspire to suggest that deeper continuities unify the world of experience despite the failures of individuals" (Ermarth, 1983: 57). In this manner Dickens typifies the realist novelist who "by successfully coordinating apparently disparate elements ... asserts the existence of a common ordering system; apparently unrelated particulars sooner or later reveal a connectedness, a pattern" (ibid). Thus Dickens produces a picture of the world, that for the reader is the one true depiction, one that the reader would undoubtedly recognise if they were in Dickens's position.

Novelistic Conventions Overturned

In a parallel to Cézanne's place in the vanguard of the momentous changes in painting (to which we come later), Henry James may be considered as breaking fresh ground in the realm of fiction. Not to be constrained by the dictates of convention, and to continue to suffer the frustrations these dictates imposed on authors in their attempts to more richly represent the changing world, James in *The Turn of the Screw* (1898/1998), undermines many of those conventions. For him "there is no realist 'objectifier' here, no superior reference frame against which the systems can be measured. In fact the absence of any 'objectifier,' of any privileged point of view, is symbolized in the story itself by the inaccessibility of the owner/employer, the absent god of the tale. There is no Providence for the reader to look to, no omniscient narrator, no empirical testing or verification" (Vargish & Mook, 1998: 46). The story provides contradictory narratives, of the insane governess/narrator and that of real ghosts, both with equal validity. It provides no one truth, no single point perspective that 'tells it as it is', despite many creative and fervent, if ultimately futile attempts to do so. If anything with this story he presents an exceptional, if implicit, disparagement of the mental rigidity that is unable to tolerate this contradiction and insists on attempting its resolution.

Bakhtin makes a similar point about the writing of Dostoevsky where he suggests "we don't have a great number of destinies and lives developing within a single objective world, enlightened by the consciousness of the author alone; rather we have a plurality of consciousnesses, with equal rights, each with its own world, combining in the unity of an event but none the less without fusing" (Bakhtin as cited in Todorov, 1984: 104). It is this heterogeneity along with the introduction of heteroglossia where multiple languages and discourses act "like mirrors that face each other, each reflecting in its own way a piece, a tiny corner of the world, force us to guess at and grasp for a world behind their mutually reflecting aspects that is broader, more multi-levelled, containing more and varied horizons than would be available to a single language or single mirror" (Bakhtin, 1981: 414-415) that helps bring a new set of values and concepts to the role of narrative.

If Henry James broke the ground for a new form of narrative, with Dostoevsky's heterogeneity and heteroglossia along with Joyce's (1914/1981) multiple narratives pointing the way, Franz Kafka could be considered as having rearranged the landscape. The publication of *The Penal Colony* (Kafka, 1919/1999a), as well as much of his other writing, presented a series of narratives divorced from the earlier conventions of understanding. Here the story is packed with possible meanings, so much so that any potential primary meaning is dissolved in the very multiplicity of possibilities. He shatters the inherent temporal continuity of earlier writing through the introduction of temporal and spatial disjunctions, until "you never know what you are going to find in your own house" and you finish before you have begun (Kafka, 1999b: 220 & 225). A particular favorite convention subject to collapse within Kafka's narratives are attempts at measurement, quantification or understanding of 'alternate' systems from within an 'other', any attempts to do so seemed doomed to failure (Vargish & Mook, 1999). In an unnerving description of the 'metamorphosis' of Gregor Samsa into a gigantic insect (Kafka, 1999c) we are provided with the implication that any attempt at the perception of reality is likely to lead to ambiguity. Thus ambiguity, derived from the (multiple) perceptions of multiple realities becomes not only a narrative technique but a constituent theme of that narrative.

However it is fundamental to make clear that this new form of narrative, does not make redundant or discard that of the old, so much as incorporates it, because essential to the strength and vitality of its nature is its very diversity. A diversity enhanced by these contributing frameworks that help serve to generate the ambiguity, multiplicity and incongruities that are part of its essence. Again Kafka (1999c) serves to illustrate this, The Metamorphosis gains its strength through, traditional realist narrative acting to describe a very 'ordinary framework' of home and family in both continuity, and sharp juxtaposition, with Gregor's bizarre transmutation into a giant insect.

These many 'distortions', in the terms of traditional conventions, preclude an easy reading utilizing their prescriptions to derive meaning from narrative, it is no longer an option to ignore anything outside these conventions as a 'misprint' or irrelevant. It is only through engaging with the multiplicities, contradictions and distortions that it may be possible to gain a better approximation of the lived human condition that these authors strive to present.

An Aperspectival Future for the Study of Management and Organizations?

Painting as with contemporary narrative has not shown the same degree of fear of rules, and the possibilities and problems it may present, as management thinking. So how may painting aid as in our search for understanding?

For the artist the persuasiveness of the image was in its ability to convey the 'reality' it represented, and for artists in the perspectival world, this could only be achieved by rigidly and religiously following the rules of perspective. These rules governed them, and their ability to persuade the viewer/observer that the picture they were seeing/viewing did indeed realistically convey the sense, and essence, of the represented object. A persuasiveness that, as previously discussed, gained much of its legitimacy through a collective collusion, about the nature of the relationship between reality, its perspectivally derived representation, and the interpretation of that representation utilizing the rules of perspective. However for some, such rules were too constraining, and seem to further highlight the limitations of the ability of the artist to represent the real. As Cézanne claimed " I wished to copy nature but I could not. But I was satisfied when I discovered that the sun could not be reproduced but that it must be represented by something else ..." (Gebser, 1984: 478).

Thus art could be considered as reflecting a more general situation in society as a whole, with the turn of the last century, it could be argued, a paradigm shift was taking place in many fields of understanding. The theory of relativity could be considered as signalling the fall of the reigning paradigm of Newtonian physics, Euclidian geometry was being supplanted by Non-Euclidian geometry, etc, and thus as Damisch (1994: 28) argues, "the following conclusion is unavoidable: just as linear perspective provided descriptive conventions best suited to that representation of "truth" prevalent in the Renaissance, "it is widely agreed [I am quoting Edgerton] that Cubism and its derivative forms in modern art are in the same way the proper pictorial means for representing the 'truth' of the post-Einsteinian of paradigm.". A position emphasized by Panofsky , who stated that perspective construction "formalizes a conception of space which, in spite of all changes, underlies all post medieval art up to, say, the *Demoiselles d' Avignon* by Picasso (1907), just as it underlies all post medieval physics up to Einstein's *Theory of Relativity* (1905)" (Panofsky, 1953: 5).

The dominance of perspectival understanding conditions the manner in which we view ourselves and the world—this is no less true for the study of management and organizations, as it is for art. Who, it would seem, perhaps because of its desire to be seen as a 'legitimate' academic discipline, proceeded down its route of prescription, measurement, quantification and yet more measurement, seemly oblivious to these threads of discontent. Taylor's pronouncements of how people were to be managed were tantamount to prescriptions for effective practice, and that the study of jobs and organizations was a 'true science'. Thus, he suggested it was possible to rationalise all activities in organizations, in such a way as to provide optimal levels of performance, and consequently was at the birth, if not one of the midwives, of this trend to squeeze the space, and the freedom it represents, from organizations. Such a view might be reminiscent of societal trends away from freedom—this was after all the predominant view of the world at the time, albeit it one that, as has just been suggested was on the cusp of change. The emergence of management during the period when the value of the control and quantification was at its zenith may have had an implicit, and apparently lasting influence on its development. As Hauser suggests "the unification of space and the unified standards of proportion [in Renaissance art] ... are the creations of the same spirit which makes its way in the organization of labour... the credit system and double entry book keeping" (Hauser, 1951: 277). A spirit, whose influence has apparently increased in the study of management while it has waned in these other fields of understanding. Yet, for us, students of management nearly a century later we now return to this cusp. We are now embroiled in a similar myriad of questions and debates regarding the effectiveness of our understanding, our tools, and our techniques, in the elaboration of management and organization studies.

We can recall in painting, Cézanne identified the inadequacies of perspective and its restrictive rules, claiming, "I wished to copy nature but I could not..." (Gebser, 1984: 478), his solution was to experiment with color in such a way as to reveal the depth and richness of the juxtaposed relationships. Picasso likewise felt constrained by perspective and was inspired by Cézanne's courage, to experiment and explore new ways of developing art. He established a form, which combined elements seen from many different angles, abandoning the traditional laws of perspective where natural objects are seized from a single angle. His painting '*The Demoiselles d' Avignon*' (1907) marked a threshold in the development of painting. Picasso was in a sense seeking to persuade the observer of the need to go *beyond* making simple comparisons with the real—but requiring the observer to almost transport him/herself beyond the actuality of the painting and immerse themselves in its potential. And to do this requires not one interpretation but many and thus we can appreciate the moving of the viewing point of the object to multiple different positions, while at the same time dividing it into many fragments, allowed the presentation of an alternative representation of the reality. He had recognized the incompleteness of his early technique, and therefore strove to surpass its limitations. This technique explores space, it "functions on a level quite distinct from that implied by the propositions of Euclidian geometry: in [this] case, space is apprehended qualitatively intuitively; in the other [perspectival view] it is conceived as a rational essentially metrical system" (Damisch, 1994: 10) Thus he transcends the rule ridden perspectival approach, and its inherent characteristics, which although illuminating selected aspects of reality, also acts to repress and minimise other aspects of the total reality. It renders visible to sight, or perhaps *insight*, that which the reductionism of the lines and rules of perspective obscures and conceals.

Picasso's 1926 drawing of a woman (Figure 3) further illustrates some of these issues, it forces us to "take in at one glance the whole (wo)man, perceiving not just one possible aspect, but simultaneously, the front, the side, and the back. In sum, all the various aspects are present at once." (Gebser, 1984: 24-25). It requires more than a passive receptivity, we must 'construct' an understanding—it demands "that we successively superimpose upon one another the various facets or aspects of the same thing, to produce finally ... the thing depicted in all its facets and thus in a new colorful plasticity" (Gadamer, 1986: 27). Picasso

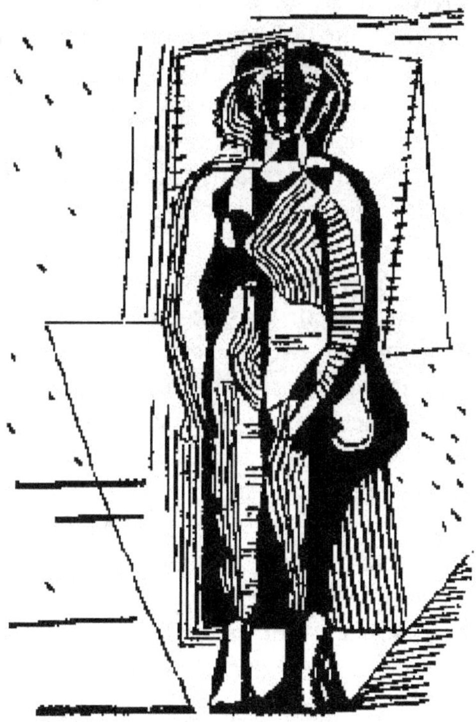

Figure 3

doesn't present an easy image, one that can be seamlessly interpreted through applying a universal set of rules. He requires us to engage with the representation, to construct an understanding. It is manifestly impossible to generate a single seamless 'reality', there is no final definitive truth, as the viewer is always aware of alternate planes, angles, shapes, and shadows that are not only not part of the current synthesis, and may be complimentary, seemingly irrelevant, or often contradictory, but can not be ignored. This inherent contradictory nature is clearly demonstrated in other works from Picasso such as *Guitar, Wineglass, Bottle of Vieux Marc* (1913) and *The Cup of Coffee* (1913) where the juxtaposition of signifiers does not "represent an attempt to synthesise different 'views' ... into a synthetic whole, rather the signifiers remain in the opposition" (Poggi, 1988: 316). Complexity and contradictions are manifest in his use of multiple planar overlays where a contiguous group of planes may serve to both indicate a given spatial recession, while elsewhere contradicting that recession. While the use of over-determination in which a single line or area performs multiple roles in representation serves to bring to the works the variable multiple perceptions prevalent in life.

Thus Picasso throws down a challenge to the seductiveness of 'ease of understanding', he makes transparent the partial nature of any representation, forcing the recognition that each viewing will be different. Through inscribing multiple "paradigms in a paradoxical play of identity and difference, Picasso demonstrated that the material literalness of the 'object' itself was constituted within a system of oppositions" (Poggi, 1988: 320). He opens understanding to the play of paradox, conflicting interpretations and the collision of multiple cultural codes. Shows that for every aspect an individual interpretation clarifies, others will be hidden, obscured or distorted. He brings to the fore both the lucidity and contradictory essence of real life, and urges us to recognise and embrace this uncertainty.

Inspired by Picasso and the other Cubists, Boccioni as well as capturing this fragmentation, uncertainty and contradiction further challenges the delimiting, delineating and objectifying tendencies of perspectival perception. Not for him the artificial divorcing of object from subject, and the synthetically circumscribed boundaries derived from the process of objectifying and spatialization. In his *The Street Penetrates the House* (1911, Figure 4) he manages to depict the interpenetrative nature of life, to subvert the conventional contrived separation of subject, object and environment, and reveal their contiguity and intercurrence. "Buildings are open forms", he "graphically depicts the penetration of noise into someone from the house ...

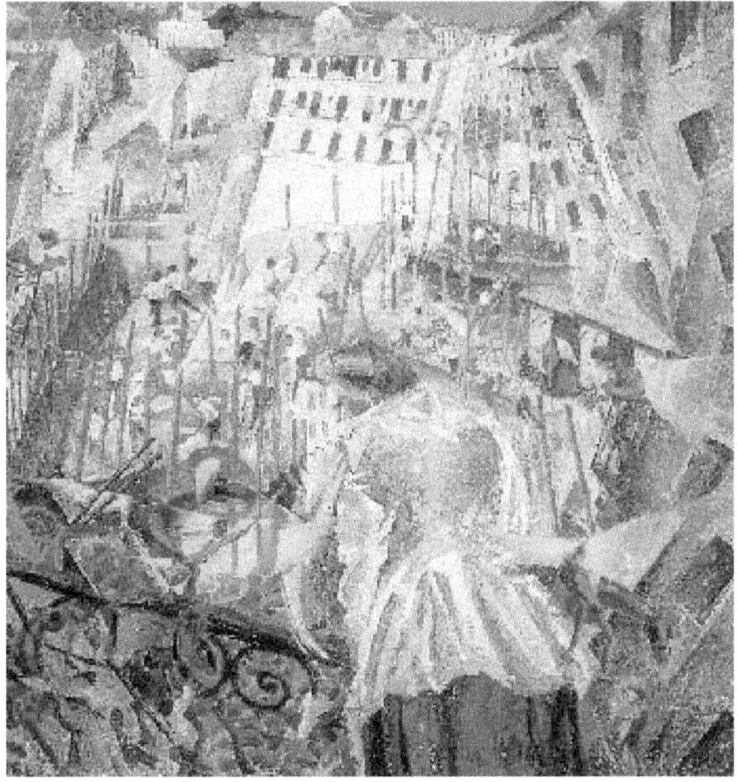

Figure 4

the material world penetrates her body as sounds and images penetrate her consciousness" (Kern, 1983: 197).

As with the earlier description of new forms of narrative, previous representational techniques become part of, and add to the value, concept and heterogeneity of aperspective. An occurrence clearly manifest in the effect of Braque's incorporation of a *trompe l'oeil* nail in *Pitcher and Violin* (1910) or Picasso's introduction of a piece of oilcloth, decorated with a realist perspectival depiction of interwoven caning, in *Still Life with Chair-Caning* (1912) to help assert the inherent multiplicity.

Our purpose in drawing our reader's attention to the experience of painting is to reveal commonality. The impetus for this paper is to expose and guard against increasing trends of measuring or illuminating only those aspects of organizational activities, which are formal or rule based. Management research has 'swooped' into organizations with promises of understanding—producing seamless representations, based on the rules of the current management fad or fashion. The persuasiveness of these representations being based on a collusion between the researcher and their self-referential discourse. Accordingly, the tools and techniques employed, the known and the unknown, remain constant and organizational practice remains partial. A partiality that too often leads to the inevitable collapse and disappointment.

Organizations are seen too frequently as 'idealized' entities—with rational beings, with clear structures, and clear relationships. Organizations are idealized as measurable, rule governed, action-oriented sets of activities—but what are they really?

Contradictions, Inconsistencies, and Heterogeneity

In our introduction we berated organizational understanding for its unthinking seduction by, and reliance on, the easy understandings obtainable through a rule informed interpretation of organizational performance. This blinkered commitment has led to a disjunction of much management understanding from the values espoused in other fields that have moved on from similar rule based simplistic perceptions. One major problem identified was the tendency for rule based interpretation to discount, ignore, or deem irrelevant anything encountered that does not fit easily within its tenets. An ignorance and dismissiveness that far too often, appears to return to haunt organizations.

In our exploration of the values of other contemporary cultural understandings we identified a very different attitude to the contradictory, distorted and ambiguous nature of much of the modern world. Perhaps it is time to learn from art and literature's desire to explore our multiple aspects and perceptions, and recognise management as a connected, related set of activities It is suggested that management research need not continue to follow a set of rules analogous to those that led painting to compliance with the strictures of perspective, or narrative to its earlier conventions of realism. Rules which serve to obscure much of reality they do not necessarily guide action—they might in fact eclipse our possible levels of understanding.

Through this paper we hope to convey our concern for the need to engage with wholeness, in a way that is not restricted, or circumscribed to these prescriptive approaches. A view that does not discount the undoubted contributions to management of alternative positions, and is thus prepared to explore new fields, that may stimulate fresh insights, which take account of the depth and richness of the actions which constitutes our present understanding of organizations. One, which does not originate with perspectives, modernism and comparisons to this particular view of the world—but which strives to take bold new steps. However it is not suggested that existing frameworks and understandings be discarded, but as with art and literature, are incorporated and developed for they are an integral part of generating the diversity, heterogeneity and contradictions that serve to stimulate greater understanding.

To take such a step is not new—we can appreciate that a similar dilemma confronted renaissance man (and woman) who might well have thought of themselves at that time to be the epitome of sophistication, and who were conditioned to this perspectival world. A world that was eventually revolutionized by among others Cézanne, Picasso and Kafka. However it is necessary to recognise many people at that time did not appreciate the significance of their rejections of these rules. Constrained by a perspectival mindset and without the conceptual tools to grasp these new conceptualizations, many people thought these artists just could not paint very well, or that this new writing was gibberish!! Our own tentative, and partial attempts to embrace these concepts bring home for us the difficulty of this leap, but again we draw further inspiration from these other fields that have succeeded despite much initial scepticism. It is recognized that this form of understanding may not appear to correlate with many 'common sense' observations, and is likely to arouse the same disdain, particularly from the general public, as did Einstein's challenging of the 'obviously observable' effects of Newtonian physics, or as in the difficulties involved in understanding Cubism, which still remain a source of humour ninety years later.

We, in management studies, are at this same point—we are aware of our dissatisfaction and this paper, might be for some little more than a target for a similar scathing reply—'*they do not appreciate this or they can't paint right, this doesn't make sense …*' It may be that our existing tools/techniques/methods are indeed sufficient, but our perceptions are at present still conditioned by our logocentric dominant logic. At this time it is not possible to grasp the significance of this call, a point of which, we as authors are all too aware, and hope that this paper may at least be persuasive as to the potential of this exciting and enjoyable field of enquiry.

For us, the incentive for these new explorations—What if the nature of reality itself is, logically inconsistent or contradictory?

References

Bakhtin, M. (1981). Discourse in the novel. In M. Bakhtin (Ed.), *The dialogic imagination: Four essays by M.M. Bakhtin* (pp.259-422). Austin: University of Texas.

Blanchard, K., & Johnson, S. (1983). *The one minute manager.* Glasgow: Fontana.

Corvellec, H. (1997). *Stories of achievements: Narrative features of organizational performance.* New Brunswick: Transaction.

Damisch, H. (1994). *The origin of perspective.* Massachusetts: MIT.

Ermarth, E. (1983). *Realism and consensus in the English novel.* New Jersey: Princeton University.

Ermarth, E. (1992). *Sequel to history: Postmodernism and the crisis of representational time.* New Jersey: Princeton University.

Fry, E. (1988). Picasso, cubism, and reflexivity. *Art Journal,* 296-307.

Gadamer, H. (1986). *The relevance of the beautiful and other essays.* Cambridge: Cambridge University.

Gebser, J. (1984). *The ever-present origin.* Ohio: Ohio University.

Gombrich, E. (1982). Illusion and visual deadlock. In F. Frascina & C. Harrison (Eds.), *Modern art and modernism: A critical anthology.* London: Paul Chapman.

Hammer, M. (1990). Re-engineering work: Don't automate, obliterate. *Harvard Business Review,* 68(4), 104-12

Hassler, I. (Producer). (1999). *Rough counting* [Radio Broadcast]. BBC Radio 4.

Hauser, A. (1951). *Social history of art.* London : Routledge & K. Paul

Ivins, W. (1975). *On the rationalization of sight: With an examination of three renaissance texts on perspective.* New York: Da Capo.

James, H. (1998). *The turn of the screw.* Oxford: Oxford University. (Original work published 1898)

Joyce, J. (1981). *Dubliners.* Harmondsworth: Penguin. (Original work published 1914)

Kafka, F. (1999a). The penal colony. In N. Glatzer (Ed.), *The complete short stories of Franz Kafka* (pp.140-167). London: Vintage. (Original work published 1919)

Kafka, F. (1999b). A country doctor. In N. Glatzer (Ed), *The complete short stories of Franz Kafka* (pp.220-225). London: Vintage.

Kafka, F. (1999c). The metamorphosis. In N. Glatzer (Ed), *The complete short stories of Franz Kafka* (pp.89-139). London: Vintage.

Kern, S. (1983). *The culture of time and space 1880-1918.* Massachusetts: Harvard University.

Kimbrough, R. (1966). *The turn of the screw.* New York: Norton Critical Edition.

King, I. (1999). Explicating performance from performing in organizations. EIASM, 6th *International Workshop for Organizational Cognition*, Management Centre, University of Essex, Colchester, UK.

March, J., & Sutton, R. (1997). Organizational performance as a dependent variable. *Organization Science*, 8, 698-706.

Miki, T. (1976) *What is cubism.* Retrieved January 9th, 2000 from the World Wide Web: www.indis.co.ip/cubism-asada/what_cubism_e.html.

Palmer, R. (1977). Towards a postmodern hermeneutics of performance. In M. Benamou & C. Caramello (Eds.), *Performance in postmodern culture* (pp. 19-32). Wisconsin: Coda.

Panofsky, E. (1953). *Early Netherlandish painting (*Vol. 1*).* Massachusetts: Harvard University.

Peters, T., & Waterman, R. (1982). *In search of excellence.* New York: Harper & Row.

Poggi, C. (1988). Frames of reference: 'Table' and 'Tableau' in Picasso's collages and constructions. *Art Journal*, 311-322.

Shotter, J. (1999). *At the boundaries of being: Re-figuring intellectual life.* Paper presented at the University of New Hampshire conference on Social Construction and Relational Practices, Sept 16th-19th, 1999

Siciliano, J. (1996). The relationship of board member diversity to organizational performance. *Journal of Business Ethics, 15*, 1313-1320.

Stella, F. (1986). *Working space.* Massachusetts: Harvard University.

Stern, J. (1973). *On realism.* London: Routledge & Kegan Paul.

Sussan, A., & Johnson, W. (1997). The impact of market/quality orientation on business performance. *Computers and Industrial Engineering*, 33, 161-165.

Taylor, F. (1911). *Principles of scientific management.* New York: Harper.

Todorov, T. (1984). *Mikhail Bakhtin: The dialogic principle.* Minneapolis: University of Minnesota.

Tsoukas, H. (1995). *New thinking in organizational behavior: From social engineering to reflective action.* London: Butterworth Heinemann.

Vargish, T., & Mook, D. (1999). *Inside modernism: Relativity theory, cubism, narrative.* New Haven: Yale University.

Chapter 3
The Power of Organizational Song: An Organizational Discourse and Aesthetic Expression of Organizational Culture

Nick Nissley, Steven S. Taylor & Orville Butler

Overview

In this research, the authors examine organizational songs, referring to songs that are created and sung by members of an organization as an aesthetic expression of organizational culture. Specifically, the study examines the organizational songs of the Maytag Company (USA-based manufacturer of home appliances) sales organization, and is historically situated during the invention and development of the washing machine technology (the early 1900s). The research considers organizational songs as a relatively unexamined form of organizational discourse. More critically, the research considers organizational songs as an organizational discourse and aesthetic expression of organizational culture—with "power to" shape the identity and actions of the Maytag sales organization, as well as "power over" consumer and employee behavior.

Introduction: Framing Organizational Song as a Form of Organizational Discourse

Grant, Keenoy, and Oswick (1998) assert that organization "is articulated by and through the deployment of discursive resources" (p. 12). With the emergence of social semiotics and postmodern semiotics, it has been argued that the definition of "text" can be broadened even further, to include cultural artifacts such as art, architecture, and music (Hodge & Kress, 1988; Kress & van Leeuwen, 1990; Gottdiener, 1995). We assert that organizational songs, similar to novels (e.g., Brawer, 1998; Czarniawska-Joerges & Guillet de Monthoux, 1994), poetry (e.g., Windle, 1994) and plays (e.g., Taylor, 2000) can be considered as a form of organizational discourse.

Also, Barry and Elmes (1997) assert that while much of organizational discourse ends up as some form of print, that which is communicated verbally is often overlooked. We would extend this assertion, to say, that the verbal—sung—discourse is nearly ignored in organizational studies, aside from the emerging works that explore the organization-music relationship (e.g., Clegg, 2000; Nissley, 2002). To better understand this unique form of organizational discourse, we turn to the organizational aesthetics literature.

First, we assert that the text of organizational song is rich with social meaning and can be analyzed in terms of what it reveals about a social context (e.g., the organizing of the invention and development of the washing machine within the Maytag Company). This idea is most evident when one considers the lyrics of organizational songs that readily express memories, histories, emotions, and ideologies—thus, making organizational discourse theory appropriate as a means for analysis. However, as Mattern (1998) points out, "music provides a communicative medium that is not simply an alternative way to say the same things that humans say through speech. Music, like other art forms, can express meanings that are not accessible through words or express them in ways that give listeners more immediate access to emotions" (p. 17). Similarly, Booth (1976: 242) asserts, "The words that go with music in songs live a life different from that of words written down for printed poetry". Booth suggests that song lyrics are an oral art, thus making organizational aesthetics the most appropriate place from which to analyze what the organizational songs tell us about the social organization.

Strati (1996) describes the history of aesthetic epistemology and the development of organizational aesthetics, noting that the German philosopher, Alexander Gottlieb Baumgarten developed the field of inquiry we refer to as aesthetics, during the mid-18th century, in response to the emphasis on rationality and intellectual knowledge extending back to Descartes. Strati notes:

Baumgarten conceived of aesthetics as one of the two components of the theory of knowledge or gnoseology: on the one hand, logic, which investigates intellectual knowledge; on the other, aesthetics, as both the theory of the beautiful and of the arts, which investigate sense knowledge (p. 216).

Strati (1999) develops this idea of aesthetic epistemology within the organizational studies framework. According to Strati, aesthetics in organizational life "concerns a form of human knowledge; and specifically the knowledge yielded by the perceptive faculties" (p. 2). Strati argues "that it is possible to gain aesthetic, rather than logico-rational, understanding of organizational life" (p. 7). More specifically, Strati (1992: 575) describes aesthetic discourse, and similarly Gagliardi (1996: 574) describes aesthetic communication. Nissley (2002) specifically considers organizational song as a form of aesthetic discourse/aesthetic communication.

Thus, according to Grant, Keenoy, and Oswick (1998), who assert that organization "is articulated by and through the deployment of discursive resources" (p. 12), we assert that organizational song—if understood as a form of organizational discourse—may inform the inquiry of the organizational researcher. In this research we begin by simply seeking to examine what the organizational songs of the Maytag Company may inform us about that organization—to answer, what is articulated by and through this unique form of discursive resource.

Research Methods: Making Sense of Maytag's Songs

This is a descriptive study—an exploration of organizational songs—of songs that are created by members of an organization as an expression of organizational culture. In this research we seek to examine what the organizational songs of the Maytag Company may inform us about that organization—to answer, what is articulated by and through this unique form of discursive resource. Methodologically, the study can be described as an "archaeological approach" (Strati, 1999: 189)—the investigation of 'fragments of organizational life' (organizational artifacts) and of the organizational cultures that have generated these fragments of organizational discourse.

Specifically, this research examines the organizational songs of the Maytag Company (USA-based manufacturer of household appliances), and is historically situated during the invention and development of the washing machine technology (the early 1900s). Due to the historical nature of the research and the inherent limitations, we do not claim to have *listened* to *all* the songs ever created. However, the research considers what is believed to be the most complete recording of Maytag songs[1], dating from the first half of the Twentieth Century. In addition, primary documents (e.g., company newsletters such as *Profit News* and *Maytag News*) are examined.

Butler (1997) parenthetically notes that turn of the century home appliance advertising was rich with reflexive commentary. For example, Automatic Electric Washing Machine Company's advertising slogan, "ten o'clock and the washing is done," while appearing to promise housewives quick relief to washday blues, actually reflected the fact that banker/founder of the firm, O.B. Woodrow, no longer had to leave the bank at 10 o'clock on Monday's to crank his family's hand powered washing machine. We shall start by uncritically telling the story of the organizational songs, inviting you, the reader, to make your own sense of it as you read; then, we present our analysis.

The Historical Context: The Organizational Songs of the Maytag Company

The Maytag Company began in 1893 as Parsons Band Cutter and Self-Feeder Company. By 1900 it was one of the leading manufacturers of a dying product. Maytag and his partners expanded into other farm implements introducing a small hand powered washing machine in 1907 to extend its factory season in the farming community of Newton, Iowa. But washing machines remained a sideline operation. Not until 1915 did washing machine revenues equal farm implement revenues. However, by 1923 Maytag had abandoned the farm implement business.

Maytag was not the first Newton factory to manufacture washing machines. Nor was it the largest washing machine manufacturer in Newton prior to the introduction of its aluminum tub gyrator washer in the early 1920s. One Minute Washing Machine Company peaked its production in 1911, manufacturing some forty thousand washing machines that year. At the end of World War I, both One Minute and Automatic Electric Washing Machine Company manufactured more washing machines than did Maytag. Several other firms in Newton and the surrounding communities manufactured smaller numbers of washing machines—some as sidelines to other seasonal businesses[2].

Yet Maytag had to transform its business and marketing plan for the "gyrafoam" washer to succeed. When Maytag distributors demonstrated their first Model 80 washers, washing clothes as they had always washed them, the clothes came out badly torn. F.L. Maytag, the firm's founder, and Howard Snyder, the firms design expert, rushed to Minneapolis to counter competitors' claims that the new machine was an "ensilage cutter" and "spaghetti machine"[3]. It quickly became clear that if Maytag were to succeed with their new washing machine they would have to rely upon direct sales and demonstrations to the consumer[4].

The 1920s were a period of growth for Newton's major washing machine manufacturers, but Maytag, after the 1922 introduction of their aluminum "Model 80" washing machine, outstripped its competitors. While industry sales improved by sixty-eight percent in 1922, Maytag's improved by three hundred sixty-one percent[5]. Maytag would double in size every year between 1922 and 1927. Maytag struggled to maintain control of its innovative technology, but not until 1931 was it granted crucial patents on its "gyrafoam" washer[6].

By 1925 many of its competitors both in Newton and throughout the United States were adopting similar washing machine technologies[7].

Maytag increased its advertising budget in the fall of 1924 to counter inroads made by competitors into the agitator washer market and sought new means to motivate its sales force. New advertising included sponsorship of the "Maytag Troubadours" who composed and sang songs such as "The Aluminum Blues," "The Rack Bar Rag," "The Wringer Rings," and "The Gyrafoam Waltz" on the new Des Moines radio station WHO[8]. At the next annual sales meeting, in January 1925, songs were introduced as a motivational tool for Maytag's sales force.

Maytag began the meeting facing several problems. The company had just finished paying off its debts incurred during World War I, in developing the aluminum washer and had established a $1.5 million dollar recapitalization program. Maytag was king of the washing machine industry, but king in a capital community. Iowa produced 60% of washing machines manufactured in the United States in 1924. Maytag produced about 20% of the nations washing machines, Newton's remaining three plants produced about another 25%, and the rest of Iowa produced another 15% of the nations washing machines. National competitors like General Electric, had between a ten to twenty percent decline in business the previous year, while the four Newton firms, Maytag, Automatic Electric, One Minute, and Woodrow, all had substantial increases. Maytag's serious competition lay just across the street, and the annual sales conventions, complete with slogans and special entertainment became a mechanism not only for boosting enthusiasm among the sales force, but for intimidating the competition.

Maytag had long held sales conventions for its branch managers, expanding them to include the newly developed sales force in 1923. Maytag's sales conventions would typically follow the week after the much smaller sales conventions of Automatic Electric, One Minute and Woodrow. The conventions were lavish affairs. Entertainment alone for the 1924 convention, hosting 200 salesmen, cost $20,000[9]. The typical convention would consist of several sales meetings, evening movies or live entertainment culminating in a sales banquet the last night of the convention. Each company would try to out do their local competitors' convention.

Maytag would begin 1925 facing problems common to many successful companies. They had just redesigned their Model 80 washer to eliminate leaks through the agitator mechanism—a problem which had enabled competitors to start cutting into Maytag's agitator washer market. Numerous competitors were contesting Maytag's gyrator patent application and potentially infringing machines had been introduced to the market. While Maytag and its three Newton-based competitors continued to increase sales, other national firms had sales declines the previous year[10]. By June of the previous year, Newton's three largest firms, Maytag, Automatic and One Minute manufactured forty-seven percent of America's washing machines. Both Automatic and One Minute had introduced new washer lines. Maytag was successful but faced new and increasingly viable competition. It had substantially increased its newspaper advertising to counter the growing competition.

At its annual convention held January 8-10, 1925, Maytag turned to songs to help motivate its sales force. On January 9, Newton Rotary Club appeared at a sales convention meeting, marching in singing "My Maytag Gyrafoam" to the tune of "My Irish Rose". The next night salesmen from the various divisions spread enthusiasm at the banquet held in Des Moines' Savery hotel by singing parodies of popular songs. "How do you do, Mr. Maytag," "Good Ol' Maytag" and "Yes, We Have No Excuses" became the standards of the evening[11].

Sales conventions quickly became more than an annual affair. In 1926 Paul Scott, manager of Maytag's Eastern Branch sales force, held a series of "It's a Great Gang that Sells the Maytag" banquets where Maytag songs became the order of the day[12]. Other branches would reward top salesmen with trips to the Maytag factory for a branch convention. Again, focusing on songs to whip up enthusiasm for both the branch and the company. Even the Lockhardt-Walker evangelistic services joined in. On "Maytag Night" Maytag employees and their families would be invited to sit in reserved seats and the singing evangelist led the congregation in singing:

"Maytag, Maytag, Maytag
Cleanest Name I Know.
Maytag, Maytag, Maytag
Washes Clothes as White as Snow"[13].

In Newton the local band would pipe trainload shipments of Maytag washers out of town to the tunes "That's Where the Tall Corn Grows" and "The Gangs All Here"[14].

On July 12, 1927, Maytag factory workers dressed in white, and wearing Maytag fezzes, assembled at the factory before marching to the community picnic grounds—singing Maytag songs. This picnic celebrated the founder's seventieth birthday, July 14, 1927, and saw the publication of the first Maytag songbook[15]. This initial songbook, included songs not only promoting the sales of Maytag washer, but also songs to shape the dreams of young consumers.

As Maytag songbooks became a common script at sales meetings, Maytag expanded the use of music to shape the culture of the sales organization. In the fall of 1927, Automatic Washer Company, taking its clue from the earlier Maytag Troubadors, began sponsoring the Apollo Quartet singing under the name "Automatic Agitators" over WHO radio[16]. Within a year, the Apollo Quartet was singing at Maytag sales meetings[17].

In November 1927 Maytag test marketed a radio program over Chicago's WHT[18]. The program was expanded the following month to six clear channel stations across the United States. A trio from the Chicago Philharmonic became the "Maytag Ramblers" and the 1927 "most popular disk jockey" Pat Barnes, of WHT served as master of ceremonies[19]. The network would eventually expand to fifty stations. Drawing on leading radio personalities and performers, the show's theme song became "Let a Smile be Your Umbrella and a Maytag Your Washer"[20] as Maytag spent nearly $450,000 on its radio budget. Maytag developed a program of specially written dramas, utilizing popular tunes performed by such bands as Ted Fiorito and his Edgewater Hotel Orchestra, Coon-Sanders and the Original Kansas City Nighthawks, Fred Hamm and his Recording Orchestra, Art Kassel and his "Castles in the Air Orchestra", and Dan Russo's Oriole Orchestra.

The half-hour long "Maytag Radio Hour" would expand and go through several transformations before it closed in 1932[21]. For a brief period it broadcast stories about salesmen or others who solved a family or life crisis frequently with the use of a Maytag washer or with salesmen qualities that made them uniquely Maytag[22]. By 1930 the "Maytag Happiness Hour" was delivered weekly over NBC's blue network. While Ted Fiorito initially conducted the Maytag Orchestra[23]; in an effort to cut costs, the show was frequently reorganized, not allowing for a stable conductor of the Orchestra. In 1930 Maytag cut it's radio budget by twenty-five percent and the growing depression forced further cuts[24]. By 1932, the well-known performers were gone, the Maytag Orchestra had gone through four directors[25], and the "Maytag Happiness Hour" played light music. The theme song "Let me Call You Sweetheart" no longer made direct connection to Maytag[26].

Maytag songbooks, however, continued to produce evangelistic fervor at Maytag sales meetings. In the 1930s Maytag sales organizations rewarded salesmen for songs extolling their performance[27].

Maytag songbooks in numerous editions were sold to dealers and salesmen for 2.5 cents a copy until the beginning of World War II. Maytag's sales organization was shut down for the duration of the War as the company's plants manufactured airplane parts and other military equipment. But Maytag remained a part of song lore. During the War, small Piper Cub aircraft were used to spot enemy gunfire and report range data to allied guns below. Known as the Grasshopper Artillery, their battle hymn chorus concluded:

So we'll give the Axis fits
With our Maytag Messerschmitts
We're the Grasshopper Artillery[28].

After the War one new edition of the Maytag Song book incorporated new songs about Maytag's expanded line of ovens, freezers and refrigerators. But times had changed. Maytag found it difficult to recruit door-to-door salesmen and the seller's market for much of the remainder of the 1940s made them unnecessary. Sales returned to the showroom floor and the workforce of Maytag trained and paid salesmen declined. Store salesmen sold more than Maytag products. Maytag advertising developed new techniques for attracting consumers to its products.

The Maytag songbooks of the 1920s and 1930s played a powerful role in uniting and motivating a sales force, unparalleled in the home appliance industry. Through song, they learned the features of their product line and the techniques that enabled them to sell it. Salesmen also developed camaraderie, among one another and with their customers who heard Maytag songs over the radio. Even when the decline of Maytag's "Happiness Hour" resulted in "Let Me Call You Sweetheart" for the show's theme song, every salesman undoubtedly heard, the following, instead of the traditional words.

Let me have a Maytag
For I love you true,
Let me have a Maytag
Then I'll wash for you
If you buy that Maytag
I will love you so,
Let me hear you whisper
I bought it for you.

Maytag songs defined for the salesmen, their role in the company, their relationship to the customer and their product's role in society. It shaped the organizational culture and the identity of the Maytag sales organization—extending from the factory to the salesman to the consumer—it bound them to the Maytag product and to each other. After considering these organizational songs from the Maytag Company, we assert that Mangham (1986) is right to point out that "organizations are created, sustained, and changed through talk" (p. 82)—or, more specifically, through song. But, where there is light, there is also shadow, so we now turn to a more critical analysis of organizational song at Maytag.

A More Critical Examination of the Use of Organizational Song as Organizational Discourse and an Aesthetic Expression of Organizational Culture

While the organizational studies literature is expanding, to include novels (e.g., Brawer, 1998; Czarniawska-Joerges & Guillet de Monthoux, 1994), poetry (e.g., Windle, 1994) and plays (e.g., Taylor, 2000) as forms of organizational discourse, organization and management theorists have made few contributions (e.g., Clegg, 2000; Nissley, 2002; Sicca, 2000) to the literature of music and organizations, aside from the intense interest in the relationship of jazz to organizational studies (e.g., Barrett, 2000; *Organization Science*, 1998; Bastien & Hostagier,1988, 1992; Hatch, 1997b, 1998, 1999; Perry, 1991; Weick, 1990). Also, while critical perspectives on music have been undertaken (e.g., Cary, 1990; Conrad, 1988; Lewis, 1991; Mondak, 1988), a more specific, critical management studies reading of organizational song is still unexplored in the organizational studies and organizational aesthetics literature.

Similar to Barker's (1999) research, our story of the Maytag Company sales organization's use of songs has a rhetorical character and a critical character. By rhetorical, we mean focused on how the Maytag organization "used" discourse—specifically, the aesthetic discourse of organizational song, to do things as an organization—especially, to create shared meaning among the sales organization, or in other words to sing their culture and sense of identity. In this section we also turn to what Barker (1999) refers to as the critical character. Barker describes the critical character as an "analysis of how patterns of discourse or language use create oppressive or overly constrained systems in organizations" (p. 23). Thus, we consider the use of organizational song at Maytag through the lens of critical management studies.

By applying the critical management studies lens to our "archaeological approach"—we consider a way the Maytag organization "used" the organizational songs as an organizational discourse. Here we will describe how the power of organizational song—as an organizational discourse—was used to shape the Maytag Company sales organization. We use the metaphor of "acting in concert" to describe this *power-ful* discourse—the power of organizational song to shape the culture, identity, and image of the Maytag sales organization.

Mattern (1998: 32) describes music in relation to power, differentiating "power over" and "power to," referring to a sense of power as domination, on the one hand, and power as a positive capacity on the other hand (e.g., power over the consumer, versus power to develop a community of salesmen). First, we will consider the Maytag company's organizational songs as a discourse with "power to" develop a community of salesmen. Second, we will also consider those songs as a discourse with "power over" the salesmen and consumers.

Acting in Concert: Organizational Song and the "Power To"

John Dewey (1934) wrote:

Works of art that are not remote from common life, that are widely enjoyed in a community, are signs of a unified collective life. But, they are also marvelous aids in the creation of such a life. The remaking of the material of experience in the act of expression is not an isolated event confined to the artist and to a person here and there who happens to enjoy the work. In the degree in which art exercises its office, it is also a remaking of the experience of the community in the direction of greater order and unity (p. 81).

Like Dewey, we assert that organizational song can act as both, a 'sign of community' and as an 'aid in the creation of community.' As a sign, organizational song reveals an aesthetic discourse that explains the culture of the organization. As an aid in the creation of community, organizational song acts as a form of communication through which the commonalities of community are created and discovered. Thus, the communicative capacity of organizational song supports the development of organizational culture by enabling and shaping the sharing of experience.

One reading, a more functionalist reading, reveals the organizational songs as an expressive strategy (Gagliardi, 1986)—a means of creating shared meaning among the Maytag organization. Certainly F.L. Maytag, the company's founder, also strategically expressed the values described in these songs. Consider, in a 1928 article in the *Maytag Profit News*[29], he asserted that the first rule he developed in his business life "was to keep on regardless, even blindly when some particular discouragement was hanging over me". He continued, "Many discouraging situations needed only one thing to make them turn out right—work, and because of this many complications disappeared before work like mist before the morning sun".

However, a critical management studies perspective offers another reading of the songs. Salesman and workers, not management and its agents, in the main, composed the subject Maytag songs. From this perspective, critical management studies reveals the songs as a form of cultural pedagogy and cultural hegemony (Lears, 1985), or as Altman (1990) states, a *discursive constitution of ideology*. Similarly, to Altman's concept of the discursive constitution of ideology, Mattern (1998) uses the phrase "acting in concert" as a metaphor for community-based political action through music. He describes 'acting in concert' as taking three main forms—each representing a distinctly different kind of community-based political action through music. The form which he labels as "pragmatic" (p. 30) describes how the Maytag sales organization used organizational songs. According to Mattern (1998: 30), the pragmatic form of acting in concert "occurs when members of one or more communities use music to promote awareness of shared interests". We borrow this metaphor to describe how organizational song, functioning as a form of aesthetic discourse, may have acted as a means of organizing and controlling organizational actions—specifically, the development of organizational identity (the identity of the Maytag sales organization), the organizational culture of the sales organization, and the actions of these employees.

It appears that organizational song served as a record of a community, by capturing the human experience of the salesmen and rendering it meaningful in the context of the Maytag Company, "creating a window into the identity of a community" (Mattern, 1998: 18). One may also consider the songs as a sort of organizational autobiography (Czarniawska-Joerges, 1996). Consider the following examples that offer a window into the identity of the Maytag sales organization. First, consider this song.

It's a great gang that sells the Maytag,
It's a great gang to know;
They are full of pep and ginger,
And their watchword is "Let's Go!"
Always on the level
Always fair and square,
It's a great old gang that sells the Maytag,
And my heart right there![30]

This discourse is a very straightforward expression of a set of espoused values—asserting that the Maytag salesman is energetic and honest. We hear similar values about 'working hard' expressed in the following song.

Gone are the days, when I laid in bed till nine,
Gone are the days, when I wasted hours so fine,
Gone and fore aye, for I wakened with a jerk,
I heard the prospect loudly calling;
Work, work, work.[31]

Also, consider the following song, sung to the tune of "Carolina in the Morning". Similarly, this song speaks to the values of the sales culture—the importance of "making the sale" ("get an order signer").

Nothing can be finer than to be a real headliner,
with the Maytag.
Each day I take a flyer and my sales go climbing
higher, with the Maytag.
I meet the smiling ladies as I approach the door
I call back again some evening and bask in their
smiles once more,
Oh! popper, I can't stop 'er, she is cleaning clothes
proper, with the Maytag.
She's going to sing more sweetly as she does here
washing weekly, with the Maytag.
If I get a chicken's wishbone any old day, I'll make a
wish, and here's what I'll say:
Nothing could be finer, than to be a real headliner,
with the Maytag
Nothing could be finer than to get an order signer
every morning.
Nothing could be sweeter than a prospect when
you meet her in the morning.
When the Monday's washing has her good and sore
And she is almost weeping, I pound upon the door.
Strolling in to demonstrate a good old "Maytag"
washer, in the morning.
Start the motor humming and a smile will soon be
coming in the morning.
When she sees it wash the clothes she can't help but
say:
"Ill take that 'Maytag,' what must I pay?"
Nothing could be finer than to get an order signer
every morning.[32]

Certainly a critical view must include some consideration of the context. These songs were from the 1920s—a decade of incredible prosperity and economic expansion in the US. However, it was also a decade of overnight paper millionaires—created in the bull stock market that preceded the stock market collapse of 1929 and the Great Depression.

Mattern (1998: 31) asserts that acting in concert may "occur in many different social settings and situations, including social spaces traditionally viewed as political, such as town halls and party headquarters on election night; but they may also include less traditional forms of political arenas ... In short, acting in concert can occur wherever music is produced and consumed". Thus, our research reveals the business organization as one more such social space.

In the Maytag Company, organizational songs were recorded in song books, sung at sales meetings/conventions, and sung on radio shows by groups like the "Maytag Troubadors," "Automatic Agitators," "Maytag Orchestra," and the "Maytag Ramblers". Mattern (1998: 19) notes that as an audience listens to music (like the Maytag sales organization audience), "they may begin to internalize some of its meaning, and it becomes part of their identity". He continues, "By expressing common experiences, music helps create and solidify a fund of shared memories and a sense of "who we are". These organizational songs appear to have created a sense of "who we are" for the Maytag Company sales organization.

Barker (1999) uses the language of "concertive control" when discussing self-managing teams and how "a self-managing system creates an environment that controls worker activity in ways quite different from the bureaucratic (hierarchical, rules-based) forms of control found in traditional organizational structures" (p. 3). We suggest that these organizational songs may be thought of as an earlier form of the self-managing technology of concertive control found in modern management. That is to say, singing these songs embodied the structure of culture and identity that salesmen had created for themselves, reminding them of rules of behavior that went with that culture and identity.

There is a particular power in organizational songs because songs are enjoyable. Enjoyment produces two effects. The first is engagement. The more we enjoy the song, the more we are drawn into the moment and the more the aesthetic experience dominates the instrumental concerns of the moment. As the aesthetic experience dominates the individual's critical functions and filters become less active, the felt meaning of the story is allowed to be accepted uncritically and unquestioned. The second effect is repetition. A song that is enjoyed for its own sake is more memorable and gets repeated (Taylor, Fisher, & Dufresne, in press).

Barker (1999) explains control in relation to organizational culture, using the concept of "generative discipline," referring to "the mechanism through which an organization's discursive formations and system of control ... become manifest in actual day-to-day organizational activity" (p. 42). He continues, describing generative discipline as a "method for 'teaching' us how to do good work in the organization" (p. 45). We found organizational song acting in such a way—a "rough draft" methodology for how to live in the organization (Barker, 1999: 47)—a form of cultural pedagogy and cultural hegemony (Lears, 1985). Consider this song about persistence.

When things are looking blue
And your volume's slipping too,
Turn new door-knobs.

If your profit shows in red,
There's no need to lose your head;
Turn new door-knobs.

Selling knows no regular season.
Look around and find the reason.
Turn new door-knobs.

If you find you're in a rut,
Getting dead as old King Tut,
Turn new door-knobs.[33]

This song tells a simple lesson about how to do good work in the Maytag organization, and that is to never give up—just keep making sales calls. There is no room for failure, just keep trying. The following piece is even clearer about the cultural expectations for a Maytag salesman.

This jumble of words is very plain, yet you'll find them true,
And they don't apply to anyone else, anymore than me and you,
Your life is what you make it, you can be your own Devil or God,
Remember as you go through life, you fashion the paths you trod,
You can build yourself to the highest peaks or drag yourself down,
Your name can be sung as a man among men or you can be a clown,
If other fellows get out and make good, then you can do the same,
Keep on your toes and do your stuff, it's all in playing the game,
Always be one of the pushers and don't let your feet ever drag,
For nothing goes but builders, in the gang that sells the MAYTAG.[34]

This song clearly communicates, there is no room for dreamers, for failures of any form—only success through hard work is acceptable.

If we take seriously the idea that songs created and reinforced cultural hegemony, we might then turn to the question, why did the songs fade away? The story we told suggested that after World War II, it was difficult to find salesmen and Maytag shifted to selling through retail stores. The implication is that the songs were only tied to the direct sales force culture and not connected to any broader Maytag culture. A more critical reading might be the hypothesis that the songs stopped working as way of creating and enforcing cultural hegemony. We have no data that provides any insight into this question, but we do have a possible story that is based on our ideas of how songs work as a form of aesthetic discourse. We suggest that the post-World War II workforce may have become sophisticated consumers of organizational songs.

Eco (1990) describes naïve consumers of aesthetic forms as being carried along by the song, unaware of what is happening. Sophisticated audiences are carried along as well, but are aware of the technique and methods used as well as being aware that the song is carrying them along. This sophisticated consumer can then be critical of the song while they enjoy it. This addition of criticality strikes directly at the power of songs we described above. It reengages the intellectual, critical filters and brings the nature of the song into question. Workers did not need to see the songs as a form of cultural hegemony, it may have been enough to simply see the blatant idealism of the songs and the contrast with the world they knew from their experience of World War II. We suggest that somehow the experience of World War II, both for individuals and for the nation, may have transformed workers from naïve consumers of organizational songs to more sophisticated consumers, and that may be part of why the songs faded from use in Maytag.

Next, we shift our focus from the sales organization to the customer of the Maytag washing machine (from identity development of the sales organization, to image development of the Maytag Company and its products), considering the relationship between the Maytag product, the consumer, and the organizational song.

Composing a Consumer Culture: Organizational Song and the "Power Over"

Let us now turn to the other use of the Maytag songs, as sales tools with power over the customers. Consider this sales song that was sung to a popular tune of the time.

Maytag Smile[35]
(Sung to tune of "Pack Up Your Troubles")

Put out your washing with the new Maytag
And Smile, Smile, Smile
While you are working with the New Maytag
Smile boys that's the style
What's the use of worrying
Never was worth while
So put out your washing with the New Maytag and
Smile, Smile, Smile.

The message is simple and clear—buy a Maytag and you'll be smiling. It takes only the simplest of critical readings to see the song as pure propaganda (e.g., Altman, 1990: 287), and it is hard to imagine the song having any great effect on a potential customer. That is there would be no effect if we assume a process of rational reasoning. However, aesthetic forms bypass rational reasoning processes, relying directly on felt meaning. The strength of the song is enhanced by playing on any positive felt meaning already associated with the original song "Pack up Your Troubles". As a modern example, think of English football fans singing their team song. The feeling from tens of thousands of Liverpool fans singing "You'll Never Walk Alone," cannot be ignored, even though the lyrics hardly make a compelling rational case.

Maytag clearly designed its Monday night "Maytag Radio Hour" to influence consumers. "The Maytag Radio Hour," the Company informed its dealers and salesmen, "is more than mere entertainment; it is a well designed advertisement that keeps pounding away at the old theme, 'A Maytag is the Washer for You to Buy' ". In its musical selections, the Company asserted, "we try to make love to the housewives of America. We play soft soothing music and sing love songs to take her back to her happiest days, days of courtship, carefree and bright"[36]. Many of Maytag's songs did hearken back to courtship relationships or promise youthful beauty through the purchase of a Maytag washer. Consider the following, sung to "Too Many Parties".

Too many washboards and too many tubs
May break your back some day;
Too many wristbands that have to be rubbed
Bring sorrow to you on washday.
But just get a Maytag and we have no fear
You will look younger in less than a year;
Maytags wash faster and cleaner we say,
So let's put a Maytag in your home today.
[37]

Let's turn to some additional examples. The Maytag Company introduced the washing machine to replace the washboard technology. Some of the organizational songs spoke to the consumer and why they should replace the washboard in their homes with the newer washing machine technology. Consider the following example, sung to the tune of "Bye-Bye Blackbird".

Bye-Bye Wash-Board[38]

Pack up all your cares and woes
I don't care where you go.
Bye-bye wash-board.
If somebody asks for you
I'll just say "Went Keflue"
Bye-Bye wash-board.

I have always found you mighty handy,
But that "Maytag" surely is a dandy.
It washes clothes, ladies hose,
Press the lever and away it goes
Wash-board bye-bye.

This is an example of how salesmen used a discourse that marginalized the washboard technology (e.g., "bye-bye wash-board")—a discourse that could be understood as creating "power over" the consumers' ideas of the value of old technology (e.g., washboard) versus new technology (e.g., washing machine).

Other songs served as a similar type of discourse. These did not marginalize the low-technology washboard; but, rather exalted the product benefits of the new washing machine technology. Consider the following example.

Queen for a Day[39]

Would you hear the tale of a weekly fear changed to
a happy sphere
By one who serves?
Washday now has lost blue Monday look.
Maytag days have made the whole world talk.

Washday is a dream;
Clothes supremely clean
When done Maytag way
Have that joyous satisfaction;
Clothes cleaned to perfection
Done with gyrafoam action,
Time for happiness and play.

Be the happy one
When your wash is done,
You're queen for the day.
Let the Maytag solve your troubles
With "White King" bubbles,

Notice how your play time doubles,
You're queen for the day.

These Maytag Company songs are examples of discourses framed by the sales organization and directed at consumers, seeking to exert "power over" consumer behavior. These discourses spoke to the inferiority of the previous technology (washboards) versus the superiority of the new washing machine technology. As well, these discourses exalted the product benefits of the washing machine technology; but, not at the expense of the previous technology.

Here we assert that these songs, sung by the Maytag Company sales organization, not only had "power to" shape the identity, culture, and actions of the sales organization; but the songs may have had "power over" consumer behavior (or, one may posit that this is the desire of the sales organization). We draw a parallel between the Maytag Company sales organization's use of song to compose a consumer culture (a culture predicated on the value of owning and using a Maytag washing machine product) and Altman's (1990) analysis of the Better Homes in America (BHA) Campaign, and what she named the "discursive constitution of ideology" (p. 286). Altman describes how BHA, "a national reform campaign during the 1920s, mobilized institutions with diverse interests in defining the modern American home and in addressing the American public as consumers" (p. 286). She continues, "BHA constructed a modern ideology of home ownership, housework, and consumption" (p. 280). This formation of consumer culture was realized through multiple rhetorical strategies, such as: dedication speeches; homemaking articles; fiction; and, non-fiction. Our research suggests that organizational song may have acted as a similar rhetorical strategy, and one may understand the Maytag Company sales organization's performance of organizational songs as the 'composing of a consumer culture.'

How much these songs were a factor in Maytag's sales is impossible to quantify. Certainly many other factors, from product design to the overall socio-economic environment also played a role. But we believe that the songs, as a form of aesthetic discourse played an important and often undervalued role. There is a power in aesthetic discourse that is subtle and does not fit well in most conventional theories of power. It is a power that is not based in the properties of the individuals involved, it is not based in the authority and legitimacy structures of the social situation, nor even in the relationship of those involved. It is a power based in the form (not the content) of the discourse. It is this idea of power based in form that is the unique focus of critical engagement with aesthetic discourse such as these organizational songs. And it is through this power, that songs are able to play a unique part in forming and maintaining aspects of organizations such as culture, identity, and image.

Conclusions

This study is not definitive; it is exploratory and intended to provoke thinking and ideas regarding organizational song as an organizational discourse and aesthetic expression of organizational culture. We recognize that much additional research is possible. However, we assert the following.

First, while Strati (1992) and Gagliardi (1996) have generally discussed aesthetic discourse and aesthetic communication, respectively, this research identifies organizational song as a unique organizational discourse—an aesthetic discourse. Second, Hazen (1993) posits, "Are organizations sound?" (pp. 20-21), asserting "As we hear what goes on in them, we learn something different from what we see" (p. 21). This study suggests, more specifically, that organizations may be sung; and, indeed we may learn something about the organization if we listen to the songs that are sung in organizations. Third, and similarly, O'Donnell (1985: 10) asserts a pedagogical significance of songs performed by workers. Thus, songs may teach us, organizational researchers, about organizational life, *and* such songs may teach workers about organizational life. Fourth, Barry & Elmes (1997) ask, "what form will strategic narratives take next?" This research suggests that a new form may be the organizational song, given its power to shape identity and image. Finally, the critical management studies lens allows us to consider that organizational songs not only have the "power to" teach us about organizational life, but they may also have "power over" our organizational lives—shaping those that participate in the song of organizational life.

References

Altman, K. (1990). Consuming ideology: The Better Homes in America campaign. *Critical Studies in Mass Communication*, 7, 286-307.

Barker, J. (1999). *The discipline of teamwork: Participation and concertive control.* Thousand Oaks, CA: Sage.

Barrett, F. (2000). Cultivating an aesthetic of unfolding: Jazz improvisation as a self-organising system. In S. Linstead & H. Höpfl (Eds.), *The aesthetics of organization* (pp. 228-245). London: Sage.

Barry, D. and Elmes, M. (1997). Strategy retold: Toward a narrative view of strategic discourse. *Academy of Management Review*, 22, 429-452.

Bastien, D. and Hostagier, T. (1988). Jazz as a process of organizational innovation. *Journal of Communication Research*, 15, 582-602.

Bastien, D. and Hostagier, T. (1992). Cooperation as communicative accomplishment: A symbolic interaction analysis of an improvised jazz concert. *Communication Studies*, 43, 92-104.

Booth, M. (1976). The art of words in songs. *Quarterly Journal of Speech, 62*, 242-249.

Brawer, R. (1998). *Fictions of business: Insights on management from great literature.* New York: John Wiley & Sons.

Butler, O. (1997). The changing gender of authority in American home appliance technology: Dishwasher and washing machine patents, 1860-1950. In: S. Chatterjee, (Ed.), *Studies in history of sciences*. Calcutta: The Asiatic Society.

Cary, M. (1990). Political dimensions of the blues. *Popular Music and Society, 14*, 37-48.

Clegg, S. (2000). The *Rhythm of the Saints*: Cultural resistance, popular music and collectivist organization in Salvador, Bahia and Brazil. In: S. Linstead & H. Höpfl (Eds.), *The aesthetics of organization* (pp. 246-263). London: Sage.

Conrad, C. (1988). Work songs, hegemony, and illusions of self. *Critical Studies in Mass Communication*, 5, 179-201.

Czarniawska-Joerges, B. (1996). Autobiographical acts and organizational identities. In: S. Linstead, R. Grafton Small and P. Jeffcutt (Eds.), *Understanding management* (pp. 157-171). London: Sage.

Czarniawska-Joerges, B. and Guillet de Monthoux, P. (1994). *Good novels, better management: Reading organisational realities in fiction*. Chur, Switzerland: Harwood Academic Press.

Dewey, J. (1934). *Art as experience*. New York: Perigee.

Eco, U. (1990). *The limits of interpretation*. Bloomington, IN: Indiana University Press.

Gagliardi, P. (1986). The creation and change of organizational cultures: A conceptual framework. *Organization Studies*, 7, 117-134.

Gagliardi, P. (1996). Exploring the aesthetic side of organizational life, In: S. Clegg, C. Hardy and W. Nord (Eds.), *Handbook of organizational studies* (pp. 565-580). London: Sage.

Gottdiener, M. (1995). *Postmodern semiotics: Material culture and the forms of postmodern life*. Cambridge, MA: Blackwell.

Grant, D., Keenoy, T. and Oswick, C. (1998). Introduction: Organizational discourse: of diversity, dichotomy, and multi-disciplinarity. In D. Grant, T. Keenoy and C. Oswick (Eds.), *Discourse + Organization* (pp. 1-13). London: Sage.

Hatch, M. (1997). Jazzing up the theory of organizational improvisation. *Advances in Strategic Management*, 14, 181-191.

Hatch, M. (1998). Jazz as a metaphor for organizing in the 21st century. *Organization Science*, 9, 556-557.

Hatch, M. (1999). Exploring the empty spaces of organizing: How improvisational jazz helps redescribe organizational structure. *Organization Studies*, 20, 75-90.

Hazen, M. (1993). Towards polyphonic organization. *Journal of Organizational Change Management*, 6(5), 15-26.

Hodge, R. and Kress, G. (1988). *Social semiotics*. Cambridge:

Polity Press.

Kress, G. and Van Leeuwen, T. (1990). *Reading images.* Geelong, Australia: Deakin University.

Lears, T. (1985). The concept of cultural hegemony: Problems and possibilities. *American Historical Review, 90*, 567-593.

Lewis, G. (1991). Storm blowing from paradise: Social protest and oppositional ideology in popular Hawaiian music. *Popular Music, 10*, 53-67.

Mangham, I. (1986). *Power and performance in organizations.* Oxford: Blackwell.

Mattern, M. (1998). *Acting in concert: Music, community, and political action.* New Brunswick, NJ: Rutgers University Press.

Mondak, J. (1988). Protest music as political persuasion. *Popular Music and Society, 12*, 25-38.

Nissley, N. (2002). Tuning-in to organizational song as aesthetic discourse. *Studies in Cultures, Organizations and Societies.*

O'Donnell, J. (1985). Industrial songs as part of a culture. *International Journal of Music Education, 6*, 7-11.

Organization Science (1998). Special issue on jazz improvisation and organizing. *Organization Science, 9*(5).

Perry, L. (1991). Strategic improvising: How to formulate and implement competitive strategies in concert. *Organizational Dynamics, 19* (4), 51-64.

Sicca, L. (2000). Chamber music and organization theory. *Studies in Cultures, Organizations and Societies*, 6(2).

Strati, A. (1992). Aesthetic understanding of organizational life. *Academy of Management Review, 17*, 568-581.

Strati, A. (1996). Organizations viewed through the lens of aesthetics. *Organization*, 3, 209-218.

Strati, A. (1999). *Organization and aesthetics.* London: Sage.

Swisher, J. (1940). The evolution of washday. *Iowa Journal of History and Politics, 38*, 3-49.

Taylor, S. (2000). Aesthetic knowledge in academia: Capitalist pigs at the Academy of Management. *Journal of Management Inquiry.*

Taylor, S., Fisher, D. and Dufresne, R. (in press). The aesthetics of management storytelling: A key to organizational learning. *Management Learning.*

Weick, K. (1990). Organised improvisation: 20 years of organizing. *Communication Studies, 40*, 241-248.

Windle, R. (1994). *The poetry of business life: An anthology*. San Francisco: Berrett-Koehler.

Notes

[1] Compiled by Orville Butler in the early 1990s, who was then affiliated with Iowa State University's Center for the Historical Studies of Technology and Science.

[2] As many as seven different firms manufactured washing machines in Newton, at least briefly, between 1900 and 1930. Most manufactured them as sideline operations to other product lines. However, four—Maytag, One Minute Washing Machine Company, Automatic Electric Washing Machine Company, and Woodrow Washing Machine Company focused on washing machine manufacturing. The neighboring communities of Grinnell and Pella also had manufacturers devoted to washing machines. (Swisher, 1940)

[3] Bones, W. (1933). *Testimony: Maytag vs. Easy & Maytag vs. Hurley and Electric Household Utilities*. Maytag Archives.

[4] High Lights of the Philadelphia Meeting of October 7th," *Maytag Profit News*, Easterner Edition, 1 (11)(December 1927): 17.

[5] *Newton Daily News*, 5 January 1923, p. 1.

[6] A 1939 Supreme Court ruling overturned those patents, but that story lies outside the purview of this paper.

[7] As late as the 1940s there were still four washboard (the manual alternative to washing machines) manufacturers in the US, and at the start of the 21st century only the Columbus Washboard Company remained, which up until 1998, was owned by Steve Taylor's (this paper's author) family.

[8] "The Maytag Troubadours," *Maytag Profit News*, Southern Leader Edition, 1 (1)(February 1927): 15.

[9] *Newton Daily News*, 2 January 1924, p. 1. *Newton Daily News*, 3 January 1924, p. 1. *Newton Daily News*, 4 January 1924, p. 1. *Newton Daily News*, 7 January 1924, p. 1.

[10] *Newton Daily News*, 29 December 1924.

[11] *Newton Daily News*, 9 January 1925, p. 1. *Maytag Profit News*, 4 (6)(January 1925): 1.

[12] "Ten Years ... A Review and a Prophecy," *Maytag Profit News*, Easterner Edition, 4 (4)(May 1930): 25-26, 54.

[13] *Newton Daily News*, 6 October 1926, p. 1. *Newton Daily News*, 7 October 1926, p. 1.

[14] *Newton Daily News*, 11 October 1926, p. 1. *Newton Daily News*, 12 October 1926, p. 1. *Maytag Profit News*, Southern Leader Edition, 1 (3)(April 1927): 18.
[15] *Newton Daily News*, 12 July 1927.
[16] *Newton Daily News*, 24 September 1927, p. 1. *Newton Daily News*, 3 October 1927, p. 6. *Newton Daily News*, 11 October 1927, p. 1. *Newton Daily News*, 8 November 1927, p. 1.
[17] "Division 'A' Marches on Newton," *Maytag Profit News*, Kansas City Spotlight Edition, 2 (9)(October 1928): 28-29, 33.
[18] *Newton Daily News*, 9 November 1927, p. 1. "WHT Radio Programs Continue," *Maytag Profit News*, Western and General Edition, 1 (12)(January 1928): 39; Bones Booster Edition, 1 (12)(January 1928): 55; Easterner Edition, 1 (12)(January 1928): 47; Southern Leader Edition, 1 (12)(January 1928): 47; Kansas City Spotlight Edition, 1 (12)(January 1928): 47; White Lightning Edition, 1 (12)(January 1928): 63.
[19] "Radio's Best Now Entertains Maytag Audience. Premier Maytag Talent Now Broadcasts From WHT, Chicago, and Five other Super-Power Stations," *Maytag Profit News*, Western and General Edition, 2 (1)(February 1928): 7, 36-37; Bones Booster Edition , 2 (1)(February 1928): 7-8, 36-37; Easterner Edition, 2 (1)(February 1928): 7-8, 52; Southern Leader Edition, 2 (1)(February 1928): 7-8, 36-37; 7-8, 52; White Lightning Edition, 2 (1)(February 1928): 7-8, 92.
[20] *Maytag Profit News*, Western and General Edition, 2 (8)(September 1928): 37.
[21] "Maytag Adds two More Stations to Radio List. Maytag Programs Now Reach Average of More Than 14,000,000 Persons Every Week," *Maytag Profit News*, Western and General Edition, 2 (2)(March 1928): 4; Bones Booster Edition , 2 (2)(March 1928): 4; Easterner Edition, 2 (2)(March 1928): 4; Southern Leader Edition, 2 (2)(March 1928): 4; Kansas City Spotlight Edition, 2 (2)(March 1928): 4; White Lightning Edition, 2 (2)(March 1928): 4. "Maytag Adds WBZ to Broadcasting Units. Boston Station Starts Programs April 6th to Cover Eastern States," *Maytag Profit News*, Western and General Edition, 2 (3)(April 1928): 6; Bones Booster Edition, 2 (3)(April 1928): 6; Easterner Edition, 2 (3)(April 1928): 6; Southern Leader Edition, 2 (3)(April 1928): 6; Kansas City Spotlight Edition, 2 (3)(April 1928): 6; White Lightning Edition, 2 (3)(April 1928): 6. "Notice," *Maytag Profit News*, White Lightning Edition, 2 (4)(May 1928): 79.

[22] "Maytag Sponsors New Type Radio Programs to on to Large Number Stations Expected to Revolutionize Our Radio Entertainment," *Maytag Profit News*, Western and General Edition, 2 (12)(January 1929): 22-23, 40; Kansas City Spotlight Edition, 2 (12)(January 1929): 22-23, 56; Bones Booster Edition, 2 (12)(January 1929): 22-23, 64; Easterner Edition, 2 (12)(January 1929): 22-23, 64; White Lightning Edition, 2 (12)(January 1929): 22-23, 104

[23] "Maytag Goes On Chain. Hook-Up with Coast-to-Coast Spread. First Program Meets with Enthusiastic Audience. Ted Fiorito and His Maytag Orchestra Prove to be Outstanding Radio Feature," *Maytag Profit News*, Western and General Edition, 4 (2)(March 1930): 18-19, 36; Bones Booster Edition, 4 (2)(March 1930): 18-19, 52; Easterner Edition, 4 (2)(March 1930): 18-19, 76; Kansas City Spotlight Edition, 4 (2)(March 1930): 18-19, 52 photocopy of Western Union Cablegram, F.L. Maytag to Roy C. Witmer, 27 January 1930.

[24] "Ten Years ... A Review and a Prophecy," *Maytag Profit News*, Easterner Edition, 4 (4)(May 1930): 25-26, 54.

[25] Ted Pearson replaced Fiorito in March 1930. Roy Bargey in turn, replaced him in May 1931, who was replaced by Clarence Wheeler early in 1932.

[26] "New conductor of the Maytag Radio Orchestra," *Maytag News*, 6 (2)(March 1932): 6.

[27] "Song Contest!!!" *Maytag Profit News*, Bones Booster Edition, 4 (5)(June 1930): 26.

[28] "Maytag Included in Song of Flying Artillerymen," *Maytag News* 17 (4)(May 1943): 12.

[29] *Maytag Profit News*, (February 1928): inside cover.

[30] "Convention Songs," *The Profit News*, 4 (6)(January 1925): 2.

[31] *Maytag Profit News*, Easterner Edition, 1 (4)(May 1927): 23.

[32] "Convention Songs," *The Profit News*, 4 (6)(January 1925): 2.

[33] *White Lightning*, 1 (2)(September 1926): 31.

[34] *Maytag Profit News*, Easterner Edition, 1 (4)(May 1927): 30-31.

[35] *Maytag Profit News*, White Lightning Edition, 1 (8)(March 1927): 12. *Maytag Profit News*, Bones Booster Edition, 1 (2) (March 1927): 12. *Maytag Profit News*, Western and General Edition, 1 (2)(March 1927): 12. *Maytag Profit News*, Easterner

Edition, 1 (6)(March 1927): 12. *Maytag Profit News*, Southern Leader Edition, 1 (2)(March 1927): 12.

[36] *Maytag Profit News*, (July 1931): 8.

[37] *Maytag Profit News*, Easterner Edition, (January/February 1926): 7.

[38] *Maytag Profit News*, White Lightning Edition, 1 (5)(June 1927): 41.

[39] *Maytag Profit News*, Western and General Edition, 3 (3)(April 1929): 24; Kansas City Spotlight Edition, 3 (3)(April 1929): 40; Bones Booster Edition, 3 (3)(April 1929): 40.

Chapter 4
On the Manager's Body as an Aesthetics of Control

Nancy Harding

Overview

This chapter stems from a larger project which aims at developing an understanding of the ways in which *managers* are subordinated to the organizations in which they work. Managers make up a large percentage of the students I teach, and I meet them often as part of my research: it seems to me that their jobs are unappealing, their amenity to being exploited is huge, but they are in the best position in which to organise some form of revolt against the conditions of their work. That they remain utterly subordinated to working lives that have little to recommend them is a source of curiosity for me. To suggest that it is their salaries or other perks of their jobs which guarantees their quiescence is, I think, crass and presumptuous. In this chapter I explore one of the reasons for their continued subordination, which I find in the aesthetics of the managerial body. The aestheticization of their bodies has been shown to be forms of control over workers (Hancock & Tyler, 2000; Warhurst & Nickson, in press): here I will develop those arguments to show how managers are similarly controlled. I am, in this chapter, drawing upon an earlier suggestion made by Hancock and Tyler (op. cit.) that combining Foucault and Marx could provide a powerful mode of understanding, but I am drawing in large part upon theorists who have developed the works of Foucault or Marx, principally Judith Butler and Fredric Jameson, to develop my arguments.

The Ubiquity of Embodiedness

Although we are only now consciously recognizing the inescapable ubiquity of bodies in organizations, the *trace* of the embodiedness of managers has been evident throughout classical management literature. Mintzberg's famous study (1973) emphasizes visibility; the empirical studies of the 1950s, 60s and 70s into the 'reality' of management, continued into the 1980s and 1990s in the work of Rosemary Stewart (1983, 1994), reveals it; and the injunction to managers to "walk the talk" embodies it. In the research I have undertaken with colleagues (Alimo-Metcalfe & Lawler, 2001; Ford & Harding, 1999) this embodiedness was encapsulated in the concept of the manager as someone who is "seen". For example, when researching concepts of leadership in organizations in 2000, we asked a senior manager in a large pharmaceutical company whether there were role models for leaders in his organization. He answered:

If you looked at our CEO, [name], I think everybody would perceive him as a leader. I am not sure everybody would think his style was the best in the world, but nevertheless they see him as a leader. He is very clear. He is out there. He is very visible. He champions the organization. I think people perceive him as a leader.

In another study of an organizational merger, we asked the chief executive of the newly merged NHS Trust, now one of the largest such organizations in the UK, how he spent his time. He first gave us a long list of the meetings he holds regularly with the senior management team, and then he turned his attention to the staff of the Trust:

I spend quite a lot of time speaking to large groups of people, larger groups of staff and managers, um open staff meetings have been a continuing need the way that we're trying to lead the organization. I'm doing one of those today at (outlying) Hospital, I did one yesterday at (even more distant) Hospital. We started to do that quarterly and we're now doing it eh twice a year, and one of those occasions is at the time we published the annual report. And that's about vis-

ible leadership and about being prepared to be accountable to the staff if you like.

His words are echoed throughout interviews with other members of the senior and middle management team. Personnel or HRM policies within this organization of 14,000 employees, the interviewees tell, revolve around the visibility of the management team and its desire to achieve emulation through the managerial exemplar.

Yet bodies remain an "absent presence" within studies of organizations (Ball, 2001). I will bring them into this chapter by, firstly, defining the way in which I am using the concept of aesthetics. I will then explore the manager's body, showing how it can be seen as an anankastic[1] aesthetic which seemingly attempts through unspoken appeals to mimesis to function as a mode of control over workers, one that my model of aesthetics suggests can be easily rejected. However, by drawing upon post-modernist and Marxist perspectives, I will show how the manager's body is both produced and consumed by the manager; that it is both subjectified and objectified; and that it thus stands both outside and inside a manager whose agentive capacity lies largely in this production of a commodity which consumes its producer.

Aesthetics

"Aesthetics" as a term is used somewhat broadly, so I will start by developing the model which will be used in this chapter. The collection of papers in *The aesthetics of organizations* (Linstead & Höpfl, 2000a) illustrates the very looseness of the concept, with authors defining aesthetics as:

- Artworks within, or the physical environment of, organizations;
- The study of organizations involved in the development of aesthetic objects;

- A research method; or,
- A form of knowledge based on the senses.

In this chapter, I use the last of the above definitions: aesthetics as a form of knowledge based upon the senses. Here, I follow Strati (2000), and Carter and Jackson (2000), who distinguish usefully between two senses of "aesthetic": one which refers to judgements about taste, where the aesthetics are a property of some object and thus are external to the individual; and the other which refers to the emotional response experienced by an individual in relation to some externality, where the aesthetics are a property of the individual rather than the externality. It is this latter sense I use to inform this chapter, which sees aesthetics as a process of knowing through tacit knowledge, and understanding achieved through empathy, which allows a contamination of the verbal by the visual and all the other senses (Strati, 2000). The aesthetic works through processes of mimesis which involve "imitating, then bricolating and innovating with the behavior and symbols of others" (Linstead, 2000: 63), so that an aesthetic response of subject to object involves an opening up to the object so that it works upon us, unselfconsciously, without the usual comprehensions of significance, meaning, interest or cause and effect, resulting in responses which are preconscious, beyond words, and therefore can clash with conscious, logical apprehensions.

But, this definition lacks a critical edge, a shortcoming partially made good by Carter and Jackson (2000) who argue that "all organization(s) produce(s) an aesthetic which is 'designed' to elicit positive responses from all those with whom transactions, of whatever kind, take place". The function of aesthetics is to mask and deny the experienced reality of organization, through a structuring of form and content in such a way as to elicit positive responses. It is an aesthetic, they say, which induces, sustains and rewards *compliance*, and works by appealing to the "shared language" of a community and the unconscious responses and intersubjective recognitions of a particular culture. To accept it without demur is to dull awareness, so "ironically, organizational aesthetics an-aesthetize" (Carter & Jackson , 2000: 195).

Aesthetic understanding can therefore be seen as *a model of knowing* which adds the sensory to discursive processes, and which can serve to mask, negate, demean and diminish. Embedded within cultures, aesthetics works upon the psyche and, carefully manipulated, can achieve subordination.

Yet there remains something amiss here, for these definitions suggest an ideology that presumes what Pollock (2001) criticizes as a "pure realm of vision that exists before gender, race, class and all other social influences have their effects" (p. 23). It suggests a subject who, although playful, is incapable of agency or of resistance to this single, shared aesthetic language. Eagleton would demur, for his work suggests that the language of the aesthetics is shared within but not between classes. He writes that:

the category of the aesthetic assumes the importance it does in modern Europe because in speaking of art it speaks of .... matters .... which are at the heart of the middle class's struggle for political hegemony. The construction of the modern notion of the aesthetic artefact is thus inseparable from the construction of the dominant ideological forms of modern class-society, and indeed from a whole new form of human subjectivity appropriate to that social order (1990: 3, emphasis added).

For Eagleton, therefore, aesthetics helps provide understanding of a subjectivity that is peculiar to the middle class. His work warns of the necessity of avoiding the presumption that an aesthetics which is a projection of a middle class subjectivity is easily incorporated into the sensibilities of other classes. Indeed, a homogeneous middle class subjectivity cannot be presumed.

The specular foundations of aesthetics, too, cannot be ignored. Whether in play, poetry, whatever, the role of the eye in the aesthetics of organizations, the eye as the royal road to the psyche, is dominant. The field of vision thus brought into play is imbued through and through with sexual difference, so that all acts of vision and visual representation involve sexuality and sexual difference (Pollock, 2001; Rose, 1986). Here, sexuality and sexual difference does not refer to "woman" (Pollock warns against the "bourgeois fiction that woman is 'the sex' above which man rises in his transcendent universality" [p. 38]) but to the fluidity of sexualities and the multiplicity of genders, the understanding given to us by gender studies and queer theory. An exploration of aesthetics must be informed by gendered susceptabilities. This raises such questions of the visual as who is looking and who is looked at, why and how and with what effects (Pollock, 2001: 27). When we as researchers step into organizations, whose imagined worlds are we allowed to see? In the wider definition of the aesthetic, we must therefore ask questions not only of the visual but of the other senses. Thus, Strati's (2000: 20 *et passim*) listing of aesthetic categories in this perspective should be qualified by a series of questions. When exploring Beauty—who defines what is Beauty? With regard to the Sublime, which "evinces the *pathos* of the material and non-material organizational artefacts that embodies the organization's memories" (Strati, 2000: 21): who decides what should be archived or canonized into memory? The Ugly—who is looking and who looked at? The Comic—who is laughing and whose laughter is suppressed? The Gracious—who is allowed to be gracious and who condemned to unnatural positions? The Picturesque or game-playing—who sets the rules, and who is allowed to break them? The Agogic, grounded in movement and rhythm—who plays the tune and who states what the steps should be? The Tragic—who gives themselves the role of hero? The Sacred, or imaginary territories such as professional competence, on which no-one must trespass—in whose interests are definitions of what is sacred maintained? Who are the high priests and who the sacrificial victims?

Furthermore, I would suggest that post-modernism has taught us that communication takes place in ways which are unintended, unconscious, accidental, etc. Thus the deliberate act of manipulation of the aesthetic which is implied in many applications of an aesthetic understanding to organizations may tell only part of the story: as we are inevitably surrounded by aesthetic objects, aesthetic forms of knowing may occur from communicating with organizational artefacts wherein no conscious attempt at instrumentalization has taken place, and where little appreciation of what has been communicated to us occurs at a conscious level.

Thus, the model of aesthetics I use in this chapter is one which agrees that organizations assail us with sensory forms of knowing and being. We may be subordinated, demeaned and controlled by them, but there is no direct relationship between aesthetic object and subjectivity. The route to the psyche has many turnings and byways; indeed perhaps it is the very playfulness of an aesthetic knowing (humor, poetics, rhythm) that allows resistance to an aesthetics the individual perceives as ugly or clashing. So although organizations, or rather their managers, increasingly seek to instrumentalize the aesthetic (Strati, 1999), resulting in gross examples of attempts at "colonizations of the idea of the beautiful as an instrument of corporate managerialism" (Hancock & Tyler, 2000: 109), the attempts may backfire, or perhaps fire off in all directions, for there is no simple causal relationship between aesthetic and its reception. Much aesthetic communication in organizations will arise without conscious intent.

The Manager's Body: An Anankastic Aesthetic

Hancock and Tyler (2000) have shown how managers may use the bodies of workers to achieve, through the use of the aesthetic of (in this case air stewardesses') bodies, organizational ends. In this section I will suggest that managers' bodies too "embody the desired aesthetic of the company" (op. cit.: 117), for they signify, using the discursive short-hand of the aesthetic, the behavior that is expected of employees. I will be focusing largely upon male managers, for they set the norms to which women managers must aspire if they are to succeed within the organization, and indeed it is possible to suggest, drawing upon ideas from queer theory, that female managers must 're-gender' themselves. I will here argue that the emphasis upon managers' visibility, upon their being seen to "walk the talk", includes within it an inchoate desire that workers gaze upon the fleshly envelopes that are paraded before them, and through gazing absorb the message contained within that envelope. The invocation inherent in the managers' bodies, a mute appeal to emulate their 'leaders', is a wish that workers become rational, logical, emotionless, utterly devoted to the ends of the organization. The aesthetic way of knowing suggests that the manager's body is an aesthetic code which attempts to insert managers into the minds of employees (Alvesson & Deetz, 1999). The code is to be found in the suit, the tie, and the enforced removal of as many references as possible to the fleshly materiality of the manager's body.

Managers' bodies are denuded, so far as is humanly possible, of all references to flesh and to nature. Clean-shaven, as much flesh as possible is hidden by the suit. The hands, perforce, must be visible, but otherwise only the head protrudes above the collar and tie. The tie has little if any practical value, but its aesthetics is Cartesian at its most profound: it sharply divides the 'head' from the (negated) body; seemingly cutting off the thinking part of the body from the flesh upon which it relies only, it would seem, for locomotion and visibility. The tie is a phallolinear mark (Reichert, 1992: 87) that divides nature from culture. Managers are clean-shaven. Hair is an ideological symbol (Synott, 1993). Rosabeth Kanter noted in 1977 that:

Managers at Indsco had to look the part. They were not exactly cut out of the same mold like paper dolls, but the similarities in appearance were striking. Even this relatively trivial matter revealed the extent of conformity pressures on managers... The norms were unmistakable, after a visitor saw enough managers, invariably white and male, with a certain shiny, clean-cut look. The only beards, even after beards became merely rather daring rather than radical, were the results of vacation-time experiments on camping trips, except (it was said), for a few in R & D—'but we know that scientists do strange things', a sales manager commented (Quoted in Synnott, 1993: 112).

Since the second world war beards have signified either rebellion or the foreign other: a clean shaven appearance signifies conformity and the conservative. Beards represent too a masculine nature that can be untamed and uncontrolled: the male is revealed as close to nature by the evidence of bodily hair that threatens to become uncontrolled if not rigidly removed at regular periods. A clean shaven chin demonstrates the suppression of nature and its elision from the controlled managerial world[2].

The manager's body is encased in a suit. The suit, J.C. Flugel noted in 1930 in *The Psychology of Clothes,* allows masculine allegiance to the larger social order and man's privileged position therein. The consequence of this, Flugel writes, is that "modern man"s clothing abounds in features which symbolize his devotion to the principles of duty, of renunciation, and of self-control. The whole relatively 'fixed' system of his clothing is, in fact, an outward sign of the strictness of his adherence to the social code (though at the same time, due to its phallic attributes, it symbolizes the most fundamental features of his sexual nature)" (Flugel, 1930: 113, quoted in Silverman, 1988: 25). In this, Silverman (*op cit*) indicates, Flugel is highlighting the contradiction between a male clothing that allows the detachment of the male body more and more from sexuality, and at the same time its construction of masculine sexuality through its phallic representation. This ambivalence is important. The be-suited, clean-shaven managerial body represents a political desire for the abstract and largely unrealizable ideal that culture and society designates as its masculine norm, expressed in this be-suited cultural production (Solomon-Godeau, 1997: 29). Yet, as Silverman (1988) reminds us, the references to sexuality and thus to nature are always there, never totally subliminated or suppressed. It is however too easy to do what Solomon-Godeau does, and argue that the continued presence of signs of 'nature' represent "the more powerful bonds that unite men to one another and which collectively operate to secure the subordinate position of women" (1997: 86), for that ignores Pollock's (2001) warning, noted above, that sexuality and sexual difference does not refer to "woman", but to "gender", and "man" is not a homogeneous category. Rather I suggest that the suit and tie, in demonstrating at once both rigid control and signs of a sexuality which always threatens to break through, can allow the manager to claim the *potential* for rampant sexuality (look at the size of that tie!!!!!!) and, importantly, the ability to rigidly subordinate and control it. Were these signs of potency totally absent, the aesthetic would lack its power.

What I will call the "social semiotics of the managerial body" (based upon a discussion in Pritchard, 2000) thus signals to workers the type of body and thus of embodied behavior to which they should aspire—ascetic, neat, disciplined, controlled, leak-proof—but always masculine and always potent. From body to mind, and here we see the power of the aesthetic—the mind that is in these bodies (Johnson, 1987) should similarly be ascetic, neat, disciplined, organized, rational, masculine. Thus the above-noted emphasis upon the need for visibility of managers and "leaders" signals the way in which managers' bodies enter the discourses of the organization and thus communicate with staff. They signify an organizational aesthetic associated with the powerful discourse of masculinity (Kerfoot, 2000), i.e., imbued with "masculine" reason rather than "feminine" nature (Seidler, 1994). "At all times", Kerfoot writes (2000: 231), "managers must be concerned with the effort to prove that they, as managerial bodies, are trustworthy and reliable; for in the accomplishment of managing their own body (sic), managers display the ability to manage others", and in occupying the "privileged bodily designations" of the manager, the "competent" manager's mark is an "ability to display the body in a manner that is culturally acceptable to their organization's bodily code". The suit is thus contrasted with other uniforms, other modes of organizational dress: the suit speaks of power and authority, of its wearer being the person who gets others to do the work.

This be-suited body is the culturally acceptable Western, Cartesian body that has well organized structures, boundaries and organs. It is a male body, one that does not leak (Shildrick, 1997). That is the message given to the senses by the manager's body. It is an anankastic aesthetic which shows that all feelings should be rigidly controlled, an excessive conscientiousness should be maintained, and a constant checking for perfectionism and meticulous accuracy should be undertaken.

This then appears to be the aesthetic of the managerial body: it (literally) embodies a shorthand version of managerial discourse, which signals to employees their encultured, commodified, objectified, subjectified status. However, I have warned above against supposing a straightforward reception of aesthetic messages. The assumption that all communications are performative, bringing into being the desired practices, is to be found in policy documents and textbooks, but agents' apprehensions of the messages are multiple, complex and variable.

Eagleton's (1990) perspective suggests that workers looking at the be-suited managerial body will react not with compliance and a desire for mimesis, but with blindness and deafness to an aesthetic that speaks a class-based language. Indeed, rejecting such an aesthetic may represent one form of resistance.

There is however one actor who cannot escape from the aesthetic of the managerial body—the manager himself. The manager looks in the mirror and sees a reflection of himself as manager. This, I suggest, is where we can see the aesthetic of the manager's body working successfully to achieve conformity, rigidity and obedience, for the manager in looking at his own reflection is the most eager recipient of its aesthetic message. This, most obviously in this Foucauldian-informed age, is a body that has been manufactured, or worked on, by the manager. In what follows I will draw upon Foucauldian theories of the body to show how the managerial body is produced as a subjectified body, and then will turn to Marx and Jameson to show that it is also an objectified body.

The Managerial Body as Subjectified Product

Implicit in the foregoing is the concept that the manager's body is not a lived body, but one dissolved materially into discourse and sign. Whilst it is important not to lose the materiality of the body (Casey, 2000), in the case of the manager's body what we see is the subordination of flesh to aesthetics, so that this lived body becomes, within organizational time and space, one constituted beyond the material. In such a constitution it becomes a subjectified body, that is a Foucauldian body whereby the material body is revealed to be a "thought body" whose particular locale in a technical, cultural and scientific history provides it with the ideas through which it is thought into being. Deleuze and Guatarri's work famously tells of a body-without-organs, a body that is experienced as a non-organic concept, not in terms of its biological organization but rather as a surface (Lash, 1991). This is a "body of inscription" and it is not the organic, anatomical body of medicine but the "non-organic, political surface". This is a social body, the body which one "does", as distinct from the body one "has" or "is" (Turner, 1992).

Judith Butler (1990, 1993) has developed these ideas powerfully. Combining Foucault with Freud and drawing upon a range of philosophical thinkers, she shows that the body is both a construction and also constitutive in that we could not operate, could not be an "I", without it, so that *construction is constitutive constraint.* She says we must ask how such constraints "produce the domain of intelligible bodies" (Butler, 1993: xi) and, following Foucault, replies that materiality must be "rethought as the effect of power, as power's most productive effect" (Butler, 1993: 2), whereby "sex" is one of the norms by which the body is qualified for a life within the domain of cultural intelligibility. Thus "the matter of bodies will be indissociable from the regulatory norms that govern their materialization and the signification of those material effects" (Butler, 1993: 2). Dealing with the unavoidable materiality of the body, Butler argues that this materiality is bound up, from its start, with signification, through the "*materiality of the signifier*" (Butler, 1993: 30). This materiality of the signifier is related, Butler argues, to a "body posited as prior to the sign" which is "always *posited or signified as prior*. This signification produces as an *effect* of its own procedure the very body that it nevertheless and simultaneously claims to discover as that which *precedes* its own actions" (Butler, 1993: 30). Here we have an analogy with the scientist in the laboratory who, the sociology of scientific knowledge has shown, claims to uncover that which was already waiting there, in nature, to be discovered, but who in effect brings nature into being through the constitutive power of scientific language. The body that Butler sees is thus brought into being through the constitutive and *performative* powers of language—the materiality of the body is prior to language, but our comprehension of that matter is achieved through signification. Here we have the familiar argument, in somewhat less familiar language, that language constitutes that which it articulates, that there is a material world but it is only comprehensible to us through language, but Butler goes beyond the familiar in demonstrating how the physical matter of bodies, which prior to Butler had been seen as beyond the reach of signification, are inevitably discursive productions.

Rose (1998), drawing upon Deleuze and psychoanalytical theory, complements this perspective of the body as both construction and constitutive restraint. The Deleuzian body, like that of Foucault and Butler, is not a "bounded envelope" containing within it a depth, but a channel of "processes, organs, flows, connections, the alignment of one aspect with another" that form a "particular body-regime" (Rose, 1998: 184). Rose suggests that the ways in which we understand our selves and our bodies at any time, indeed any distinction between the two, is because of "the ways in which particular relations of the exterior have been invaginated, folded, to form an inside to which it appears an outside must always make reference" (Rose, 1998: 188). In arguments similar in some respects to Linstead's (2000) understanding of how aesthetics operates. Linstead (2000) argues that we have become psychological creatures because of "the ways in which, in so many locales and practices, psy vectors have come to traverse and link up these machinations" (p. 185). The metaphor of the fold, which calls to mind the further metaphor of the amoeba, "describes a figure in which the inside, the subjective, is itself no more than a moment, or a series of moments, through which a 'depth' has been constituted within human being. The depth and its singularity, then, is no more than that which has been drawn in to create a space or series of cavities, pleats, and fields, which exist only in relation to those very forces, lines, techniques, and inventions that sustain them" (Linstead, 2000: 188). A configuration of forces, bodies, buildings and techniques hold in place that which has been folded inside and stabilized.

For Butler, such folding includes the physical materiality of bodies; for Rose it includes those things that at any time have authority. With regard to managers, I suggest that what is folded within the manager's body is the organization "itself", for the mimetic relationship between the human body and organization theory cannot be missed. The urge of physiologists to define and delineate is replicated by organizational theorists. This anthropomorphization, this "elision between organization and organism" (Dale & Burrell, 2000: 21) goes far beyond the status of metaphor claimed for it by Døving (1996), for the organization-as-body is not enfleshed, it is an "organ without bodies" (Dale & Burrell, 2000: 21), without emotions, perhaps even a non-human cyborg or human machine system (Parker, 2000). Importantly, the other of organization is chaos: the organization is order, harmony, control—it is not-chaos.

The mimetic relationship between organization and body is prefigured in Mary Douglas' (1966) analysis of "dirt". The boundaries of the body, she suggests, anticipating post-modern theories by more than two decades, are drawn not by the material but by the limits of the social. So great is the necessity for controlling the body that the transcendence of its boundaries is for Douglas the quintessential metaphor of social disorder and chaos. Douglas writes "each culture must have its own notions of dirt and defilement which are contrasted with its notions of the positive structure which must not be negated" (1966: 159). Furthermore, Butler (1993) suggests that a post-structuralist appropriation of Douglas' view might well understand the boundaries of the body as the limits of the socially *hegemonic*. From this perspective the manager's body can be seen as synecdochal for the social system *per se*, as a site in which open systems converge, so any kind of unregulated permeability constitutes a site of pollution and endangerment. In societies dominated by organizations, therefore, notions of "dirt and defilement" resolve themselves around notions of chaos: cleanliness signifies order; dirt its other. The be-suited managerial body, hiding away all flesh save for face and hands, clean-shaven and strictly barbered, can be seen as rigorously sweeping away all signs of "dirt" and elevating the "cleanliness" of order over the "dirt" of chaos. So, I am arguing, the manager's body speaks of the fear of unregulated workers who, if they united, could endanger the organization. However, I have suggested that workers are more or less impervious to this message, so which "unregulated worker" is to be feared?

Let me introduce at this point Foucault's concept of dressage, as used by Jackson and Carter (1998). They link two themes from the work of Foucault: governmentality and labor as dressage. Governmentality, of course, concerns the management of a population at both an aggregate and a micro level, while dressage is one of three functions of labor identified by Foucault (the other two being the productive and the symbolic). Dressage means both discipline and taming, and generally refers to the mastering of a horse in deportment and response to controls. It means "making horses perform unnatural movements and obey control which is for control's sake, for the gratification of the controller" (Jackson & Carter, 1998: 54). Labor thus, in its dressage sense, is "non-productive, non-utilitarian and unnatural behavior for the satisfaction of the controller and as a public display of compliance, obedience to discipline" (Jackson & Carter, 1998: 54). Management, charged with controlling workers but in the absence of any evidence that they need control, instigates labor as dressage, where work is subject to control, not for functional reasons but for the sake of control itself.

I suggest that managers too are subject to their labor as dressage, where they must be controlled *for the sake of control itself.* For who manages the managers? Do we not have here the internalized Panopticon, with managers managing their selves? The manager, putting on his tie in front of the mirror every morning, dressing himself up as manager, inscribing upon this be-suited body the aesthetic of order, thus becomes inscribed within a discourse of self-control, symbolized aesthetically through the peculiar artwork of the managerial body. This is an artwork that the manager appears to have fashioned himself, but in putting on his suit each weekday morning he follows a century-long fashion, seen in management textbooks in photographs of F. W. Taylor, Max Weber, Frank Gilbreth and the other "classical" managerial theorists. The perpetuation of this one fashion says much: in Derrida's (1995) terms, we see here the power of the archive. In *Archive Fever* (1995) he interweaves a complex relationship between the archive of the library or museum and that of the psyche. The archive is built through a "power of consignation" (Derrida, 1995: 3), where consignation refers to not only a putting in reserve but also "the act of *con*signing through *gathering together signs*" (Derrida, 1995: 3). Those things, not always discursive writings, stored in archives are kept and so classified by virtue of a privileged topology, "a place of election where law and singularity intersect in privilege. At the intersection of the topological and the nomological, of the place and the law, of the substrate and the authority, a scene of domiciliation becomes at once visible and invisible" (Derrida, 1995: 3). The signs consigned to the archive of the library imbricate the signs consigned to the archive of the psyche, and vice versa. The archive of the organization, from this Derridean perspective, is one which contains laws which work upon the psyche, which suppress and repress as they form and reform. In this light, the archive of the organizational aesthetic is written upon the clean shaven, be-suited managerial body, a representation that has remained largely unchanged through a century of managerial history. The imprint of the organization's history is stored and embodied in the manager's physical appearance. The aesthetic of control represented in that suit and that clean-shaven body is an aesthetic of control over managers; the manager is imprisoned within a conservative aesthetic that locks him within the ever-recycled rules and the cultures of early-20th century organizations.

The Managerial Body as Objectified Product

That then, I suggest, is the subjectified body of the manager, one which states to the manager, every time he looks in the mirror, "this is who you are; this is what you have [literally] made of yourself". In Butler's terms, it is a performative body achieved within citational practices which both enable and discipline subjects. But this is where Butler's analysis fails us, for the constitutive constraints of the gendered body differ from those operating within organizations. Nowhere in her account is there space for exploring how capitalism both constitutes and constrains. It is time therefore to take up Hancock and Tyler's (2000) hint of the possible fruitfulness of combining Foucault with Marx. Stronger hints of the utility of such a combination are now emerging within critical management literature (O'Doherty & Willmott, 2001), and in theories of the body in lived space (Harvey, 1998; Smith & Doel, 2001). Fredric Jameson has however been arguing the merits of such a combination for more than a decade, and it is to his theoretical perspective that I will turn in order to introduce a Marxist analysis of the objectified body[3]. Jameson's analysis does not explore issues relating to embodiment, so I will incorporate ideas from the sociology of the body into a Jamesonian perspective, to explore how bodies are produced under capitalism. This allows a reconciliation of the producer/consumer binary, and facilitates the re-introduction of Marx's theory of alienation, so leading to a more nuanced understanding of the aesthetic of the subjectified/objectified manager's body.

Post-modernism, for Jameson (1991: xii), is "not the cultural dominant of a wholly new social order ..., but only the reflex and the concomitant of yet another systemic modification of capitalism itself". This modification has resulted in post-modern capitalism, in Jameson's view the purest form of capital yet to emerge. Everything now has become a commodity, and by its transformation into a commodity, a thing of whatever type has been reduced to a means for its own consumption, so that "immanent intrinsic satisfactions" (Jameson, 1992: 11) from activities are lost as everything becomes means to an end. Here, where modernism could "critique the commodity and the effort to make it transcend itself," (Jameson, 1991: 1), post-modernism is the "consumption of sheer commodification as a process" (*ibid.*). The reach of this form of capitalism is vastly extended: it is globalized so that it reaches outwards, but it has also, crucially, moved into previously uncommodified areas including a colonization of the unconscious, whereby everything in our social lives is penetrated by capitalism. Significantly for this current analysis, this stage of capitalism is essentially aesthetic and located within the "single protean sense" (Jameson, 1992: 1) of the visual, so much so that were an ontology of this "artificial, person-produced universe" (Jameson, 1992: 1) still possible, it would have to be an "ontology of the visual, of being as the visible first and foremost, with the other senses draining off it; all the fights about power and desire have to take place here, between the mastery of the gaze and the illimitable richness of the visual object" (Jameson, 1992: 1). It is thus through the visual that post-modern capitalism is able to penetrate into the psyche, and it is the psyche which is the locus where individuals transform themselves into commodities designed for their own consumption.

There are no references to the aesthetics of the body in Jameson's work, but writers within the sociology of the body have developed similarly Baudrillardian-inspired ideas to show how the body is achieved through commodification and consumption. Falk (1994), for example, argues that the body is profoundly connected with the sense of self—"I consume therefore I am". It has become an outward sign of inward moral standing (Lupton, 1995) and, most influentially, a bearer of symbolic value (Shilling, 1993). The body within consumer culture, Shilling proposes in an argument which complements Jameson's, is increasingly central to self-identity, related to reflexively, and a project to be worked on, constructed, and consumed.

The sociology of the body lacks the vital political dimension added by Jameson, but the overlap between the objects of their analysis, cultural products and the psyche in Jameson's case, the commodified, constituted body within sociology of the body, suggests the two perspectives can be fruitfully united. This union produces a body that is (a) constructed and consumed within a capitalist economy whereby bodies are used in the undertaking of the role of worker in the production of goods and services and so contribute to surplus value, and (b) as consumer of capitalist goods which maintain and constitute the commodified body, and so contribute to profits. In the organization we thus have the conflation of consumption and production of *managerial bodies*, for as I have shown, the production of his/her managerial body is one of the manager's major tasks. This provides the opening whereby we can introduce Marx's theory of alienation.

Was Marx's account of the estranged laborer as potent when written as it is now, when the lens of psychological discourses (Rose, 1989) predispose our reading towards the construction of a particular type of narrative? Certainly, object-relations theory (Bollas, 1993, 1995) powerfully buttresses Marx's assertion (1986) that the product of one's labor is part of one's "essential being", a being that is confirmed by one's work. For Marx, capitalism estranges the product of one's labor, and thus both commodifies and alienates the worker. The,

object which—labor's product—confronts it as something alien, *as a* power independent *of the producer. The product of labor is labor which has been embodied in an object, which has become material: it is the* objectification *of labor. Labor's realization is its objectification. Under these economic conditions this realization of labor appears as* loss of realization *for the workers; objectification as* loss of the object and bondage to it, *appropriation as* estrangement, as alienation. (Marx, 1986: 38, emphasis in the original)

The worker "places his life in the object", but the estrangement of the object results in the alienation of the worker.

The alienation *of the worker in his product means not only that his labor becomes an object, an* external *existence, but that it exists* outside him, *independently, as something alien to him, and that it becomes a power on its own confronting him. It means that the life which he has conferred on the object confronts him as something hostile and alien.* (op. cit.: 38, emphasis in the original)

Compare this with Bollas' (1993, 1995) theory of the self, located within a post-modernist object-relations theory which sees the self as a set of idiomatic selves which depend upon significant objects for their elaboration. In Bollas' words, the self is an "internal object" that is "fashioned from several sources: from an inner feel of the authorizing aesthetic that gives polysemous (not unitary) shape to one's being; from an inner feel of internal objects which are the outcome of the other's effect upon one's self; from the shape of discrete episodes of self experience" (Bollas, 1995: 173). This "internal object", this "phenomenon of the real", is, he argues, the result of our moving through our lives as a unique set of evolving theories that generate insights and new perspectives about ourselves (Bollas, 1995: 69). The theories arise from the effect of objects upon us: people, music, artworks, artefacts, whatever, they "move through" us like ghosts, inhabiting our minds, and conjured up when we evoke their names (Bollas, 1993: 56-57) as we may do in the conscious or unconscious thought processes through which we dream ourselves into being. Thoughts of objects indeed form countless trains, thousands of ideational routes, leading to an explosive creation of meanings which meet up with new units of life experience (Bollas, 1995: 55).

There is potential in Bollas' work to develop a "bodily real" (Campbell, 2000), and there is also the potential to turn his work towards more critical ends. Bollas' version of object-relations theory can bring Marx's theory of alienation into an epoch where psychoanalytical theories form dominant constitutive discourses, and Marxist theories can radicalize Bollas' perspective. The workplace can, indeed must, contribute to those highly condensed psychic textures which allow us to be "substantially metamorphosed by the structure of objects; internally transformed by objects that leave their traces within us" (Bollas, 1993: 59). Thus what we produce in the world of work becomes part of those 'objects' which form any core sense of who we are. This core sense, Marx tells us, is alienated from us so as to achieve the ends of capitalism. Such a concept of a "core" self seemingly contradicts post-modernist ideas about the self, and indeed Jameson notes that Marx's alienated self has been replaced by a post-modernist fragmented self which has no "core" from which to be alienated. However, the trace of the cohesive, modernist self remains, and so there is the possibility of a self that is alienated from that trace. Indeed perhaps this is the inevitable outcome of the consuming society of post-modern capitalism: rather than the modernist core self we have today fragmented, post-modernist, embodied selves which include within their "fragments" a self which will stand "outside", observe and control us.

To return to the manager - we see here an employee who spends much time and effort in perfecting the managerial body, a body symbiotic with and symbolic of the organization and thus different from other workers' bodies. This managerial body is the product of the manager's labor, an object for the specular consumption of others in the organization. This is a body bound up with concepts of the self of the manager, and devoted to the ends of the organization and thus to capitalism. This is a body/self, in Marx's terms, that stands 'outside' the producer, to confront and oppress him/her. This, I would suggest, is utter alienation, for here it is my body which I, the manager, have constituted, and which now stands before me and controls me.

Conclusion: The Aesthetic of the Subjectified-Objectified Body

For Butler it is not the matter of bodies that matters, but how we constitute that matter. Where capitalism enchants managers into fashioning the matter of their bodies to capitalism's own ends, where those bodies both work in capitalism's workplaces as objectified bodies and constitute and consume themselves as subjectified bodies, those bodies become, in Marx's terms, alienated and thus capable of standing 'outside' the manager and controlling him/her. These subjectified/objectified bodies serve a particular role in the highly aestheticized world of postmodern capitalism. Where others have argued that capitalism uses beautiful bodies as part of the tools of the workplace, I argue that capitalism also uses the power of the aesthetic to render bodies into internalized forms of control. Where many workers may perhaps refuse to conform to such modes of control, managers are unable to resist. Stepping into the subject position of manager means putting on the suit, the tie and the organization, and subjecting the managerial self to the utter subjection of being controlled by that very body which, we traditionally assume, is the locus of the self.

References

Alimo-Metcalfe, B., & Lawler, J. (2001). Leadership development in British Companies at the beginning of the 21st Century: Lessons for the NHS? *Journal of Management in Medicine. 15,* 387-404.

Alvesson, M., & Deetz, S. (1999). *Doing critical management research.* London: Sage.

Ball, K. (2001, November). *Incorporating organization: Discourse, body and technology at work* Paper given at ESRC Workshop on New organizational thinking: Aesthetics, consumption, embodiment, performativity. Manchester, England.

Bollas, C. (1993). *Being a character: Psychoanalysis and self experience.* London: Routledge.

Bollas, C. (1995). *Cracking up: The work of unconscious experience.* London: Routledge.

Butler, J. (1990). *Gender trouble: Feminism and the subversion of identity.* London: Routledge

Butler, J. (1993). *Bodies that matter.* New York: Routledge.

Campbell, J. (2000). *Arguing with the phallus: Feminist, queer and postcolonial theory, a psychoanalytic contribution.* London: Zed.

Carter, P., & Jackson, N. (2000). An-aesthetics. In S. Linstead & H. Höpfl (Eds.), *The aesthetics of organization* (pp. 180-196). London: Sage.

Casey, C. (2000). Sociology sensing the body: Revitalizing a dissociative discourse. In J. Hassard, R. Holliday & H. Willmott (Eds.), *Body and organization* (pp. 52-70). London: Sage.

Dale, K., & Burrell, G. (2000). What shape are we in? Organization theory and the organized body. In J. Hassard, R. Holliday & H. Willmott (Eds.), *Body and organization* (pp. 15-30). London: Sage.

Derrida, J. (1995). *Archive fever: A Freudian impression* (E. Prenowitz, Trans.). Chicago: University of Chicago.

Douglas, M. (1966). *Purity and danger.* London: Routledge.

Døving, E. (1996) In the image of man: Organizational action, competence and learning. In D. Grant & C. Oswick (Eds.), *Metaphor and organization* (pp. 185-199). London: Sage.

Eagleton, T. (1990). *The ideology of the aesthetic.* Oxford: Blackwell.

Falk, P. (1994). *The consuming body.* London: Sage.

Ford, J., & Harding, N. (1999, July). *The psychological contract: A tool of HRM or a Faustian contract between the organisational devil and the unfree employee.* Paper presented at Standing Conference on Organizational Symbolism. Edinburgh.

Hancock, P., & Tyler, M. (2000). "The look of love": Gender and the organization of aesthetics. In J. Hassard, R. Holliday & H. Willmott (Eds.), *Body and organization* (pp. 108-129).

London: Sage.

Harvey, D. (1998). The body as an accumulation strategy. *Environment and Planning: Society and Space, 16*, 401-421.

Jackson, N., & Carter, P. (1998). Labour as dressage. In A. McKinlay & K. Starkey (Eds.), *Foucault, management and organization theory* (pp. 49-64). London: Sage.

Jameson, F. (1991). *Postmodernism, or, the cultural logic of late capitalism.* London: Verso.

Jameson, F. (1992). *Signatures of the visible.* London: Routledge.

Johnson, M. (1987). *The body in the mind: The bodily basis of meaning, imagination and reason.* Chicago: University of Chicago.

Kerfoot, D. (2000). Body work: Estrangement, disembodiment and the organizational 'other'. In J. Hassard, R. Holliday & H. Willmott (Eds.), *Body and organization* (pp. 230-246). London: Sage.

Lash, S. (1991). Genealogy and the body: Foucault/Deleuze/Nietzche. In M. Featherstone, M. Hepworth & B. Turner (Eds.), *The body: Social process and cultural theory* (pp. 256-280). London: Sage.

Linstead, S. (2000). Ashes and madness: The play of negativity and the poetics of organization. In S. Linstead & H. Höpfl (Eds.), *The aesthetics of organization* (pp. 61-92). London: Sage.

Linstead, S., & Höpfl, H. (2000). Introduction. In S. Linstead & H. Höpfl (Eds.), *The aesthetics of organization* (p. 1). London: Sage.

Lupton, D. (1995). *The imperative of health.* London: Sage.

Marx, K. (1986). *Karl Marx. A reader* (J. Elster, Ed.). Cambridge: Cambridge University.

Mintzberg, H. (1973). *The nature of managerial work.* New York: Harper and Row.

O'Doherty, D., & Willmott, H. (2001). Debating labour process theory: The issue of subjectivity and the relevance of poststructuralism. *Sociology, 35*, 457-476.

Parker, M. (2000). Manufacturing bodies: Flesh, organization, cyborgs. In J. Hassard, R. Holliday & H. Willmott (Eds.), *Body and organization* (pp. 71-86). London: Sage.

Pollock, G. (2001). *Looking back to the future: Essays on art, life and death.* Amsterdam: G & B Arts.

Pritchard, C. (2000). The body topographies of education management. In J. Hassard, R. Holliday & H. Willmott (Eds.),

Body and organization (pp. 147-165). London: Sage.

Reichert, D. (1992). On boundaries. *Environment and Planning: Society and Space, 10,* 87-98.

Rose, J. (1986). *Sexuality and the field of vision.* London: Verso Books.

Rose, N. (1989). *Governing the soul: The shaping of the private self.* London: Routledge.

Rose, N. (1998). *Inventing our selves.* Cambridge: Cambridge University.

Seidler, V. (1994). *Unreasonable men: Masculinity and social theory.* London : Routledge.

Shildrick, M. (1997). *Leaky bodies and boundaries.* London: Routledge.

Shilling, C. (1993). *The body and social theory.* London: Sage.

Silverman, K. (1988). *The acoustic mirror: The female voice in psychoanalysis and cinema.* Bloomington, IN: Indiana University.

Smith, R., & Doel, M. (1998). Baudrillard unwound: The duplicity of Post-Marxism and deconstruction . *Environment and Planning: Society and Space, 19,* 137-159.

Solomon-Godeau, A. (1997). *Male trouble. A crisis in representation.* London: Thames and Hudson .

Stewart, R. (1983). Managerial behaviour: How research has changed the traditional picture. In M. Earl (Ed.), *Perspectives in management* (pp. 82-98). Oxford: Oxford University.

Stewart, R., Barsoux, J., Kieser, A., Ganter, H., & Walgenbach, P. (1994). *Managing in Britain and Germany.* Basingstoke: St.Martin's.

Strati, A. (1999). *Organization and aesthetics.* London: Sage.

Strati, A. (2000). The aesthetic approach in organization studies. In S. Linstead & H. Höpfl (Eds.), *The aesthetics of organization* (pp. 13-34). London: Sage.

Synott, A. (1993) *The body social: Symbolism, self and society.* London: Routledge.

Turner, B. (1992). *Regulating bodies.* London: Routledge.

Warhurst, C., & Nickson, D. (in press). Rethinking aesthetics, organization and labour. *Organization.*

Notes

[1] The anankastic personality disorder is the medical name for anal retention. It is a personality disorder characterised by feelings of personal insecurity, doubt and incompleteness leading to excessive conscientiousness, checking, stubbornness and caution. There may be insistent and unwelcome thoughts or impulses which do not attain the severity of an obsessional neurosis. There is perfectionism and meticulous accuracy and a need to check repeatedly in an attempt to ensure this. Rigidity and excessive doubt may be conspicuous. (Summary of definition in *International classification of diseases, injuries and causes of death* (9th Ed), published in A *glossary of mental disorders and mental health legislation*, Wyeth Laboratories, 1980.)

[2] In the above-mentioned study of one of the NHS' largest trusts, none of the 26 managers interviewed has worn facial hair, but about 20% of the doctors have done (one also wears his hair in a pony tail). Other doctors distinguish themselves from managers by wearing bow ties or other flamboyant signifiers of an authority that allows them to refuse to be controlled. The last resort is, of course, the stethoscope.

[3] Jameson was dismissive of Foucault and preferred a Baudrillardian explication of post-modernism, a perspective which does not contradict the arguments of this paper, but rather assists in their development.

Chapter 5
An-Aesthetics and Architecture

Karen Dale & Gibson Burrell

Labour produces works of wonder for the rich, but nakedness for the worker. It produces palaces, but only hovels for the worker; it produces beauty, but cripples the worker; it replaces labour by machines but throws a part of the worker back to a barbaric labour and turns the other part into machines. It produces culture, but also imbecility and cretinism for the worker (Marx, 1844/1972).

Overview

We consider it important to look at the built environment from the standpoint of critical management studies and ask how buildings contribute to the ideological, political and economic structures of domination. The paper begins by asking what is meant by 'aesthetics'. Using the work of Wolfgang Welsch (1997) and acknowledging his dependence on Theodor Adorno (1991/2001) we can see how polysemous the concept is. But hidden away in Welsch are a very few yet suggestive references to 'anaesthetics'. The paper, in part, seeks to develop this notion. Using Huxley's *Brave New World* we can detect within the Foreword what is tantamount to an ironic manifesto for anaesthetization. We compare aesthetics with anaesthetics in the context of architecture and attempt to show how the "dazzle" (Benjamin, circa 1930s/1999) of buildings is often accompanied by desensitisation of those who live and work within them. This is to say that almost every aesthetic development is matched with an anaesthetizing one. Sometimes this is only at the level of the individual sensorium but often those who designed the dazzle, those who produced the dazzle and those who provided the raw materials for the dazzle face intense desensitisation in order to produce the 'phantasamagoria' of which Walter Benjamin (circa 1930s/1999) spoke. The paper critiques an article by Mauro Guillen (1997) who sees Taylorism as an aesthetic and in so doing gives brief consideration to the 'zero architecture' (Banham, 1986) of Albert Kahn's factories and the work of Skidmore, Owings and Merrill whom are seen as the 'utilitarian heirs' to Kahn, in the realm of office design for corporate capitalism. Whilst corporate owners may well see these buildings as 'phantasamagoria', for those who work in them all that is offered is anaesthesia.

What is Aesthetics?

Wolfgang Welsch (1997) maintains that 'the aesthetic' is a polysemy in that there is a wide variety of usages of the term circulating which, although inter-related, do give one quite distinct perspectives on the topic. Some of these are as follows:

- The measurement and appreciation of the beautiful—callistics;
- The appreciation of good design and that which provides good form, i.e., cosmetics;
- The ability to makes a harmonious appealing whole from disparate elements;
- The ability to perceive contrasts between contiguous elements, e.g., color;
- The appreciation of the sensuous—that which appeals to all the senses;
- The appreciation of that which requires the higher cultivated senses;
- That which requires perceptiveness rather than sensateness;
- That which requires time to appreciate and is beyond the immediacy of the moment;

- That which concerns itself with phenomenological appearance and not substance, and
- The ability to draw all the above elements into one piece of artistic creation;

We find this helpful as a way of gaining purchase on the slipperiness of the term 'aesthetics', but what we find even more useful is a very minor point hidden away within the book. Welsch goes on, in one or two isolated spots within the text (1997: 25, 72, 83), to raise the issue of the 'double figure' of aesthetics and anaesthestics. Is he suggesting then that the opposite of aesthetics is anaesthetics? Partly. This point is also made in part by Antonio Strati (1999: 81). Aesthetics, says Strati, is the knowledge given to us by our sensory organs and is related to the Greek verb "*aisth*" which means "to feel". It is thus very different from theological disputation about meaning. It can be seen, says Strati (*ibid.*), as "the sensibilities activated to help humans observe, just as anaesthetics' ... is the means whereby the sensory facilities are blunted, and one of these means may be art". In other words, art may stimulate sensibility into insensibility by transforming the 'everyday' into the 'special' by decoration, hedonism and the creation of illusion. "These are ways to 'anaethetise' organizational actors and thereby render them insensitive and entirely unable to comprehend organizational life" (ibid.). So, for Strati, whilst aesthetics sharpens the sensory faculties (sic), anaesthetics dulls them (sic).

Welsch (1997) too, says that continued excitement leads to indifference. Over-stimulus gives way to the nervous system shutting down, nothing seems beautiful anymore and the sensuous gives way to desensitization. The globalization of the aesthetic means that ubiquitous beauty loses its appeal and its meaning. If beauty is everywhere it can even become terrifying. But at this point Welsch differs from Strati. For, to the extent that one or more of the senses is stimulated through an aesthetized stimulus it is implied that one or more of the remaining senses is anesthetized. Welsch sees the human sensorium as a bundle of different senses undergoing differing levels of sensory stimulation whilst Strati rolls them all in together. The privileging of the visual, we might infer from this, can lead to the terror of loss of perceptive feeling in the auditory or the olfactory senses. Anaesthetization thus can become one way of surviving the terror of partial stimulation or over-stimulation of the senses and of perception.

We would like to take the concept of *anaesthetization* somewhat further and infuse it with more of a political flavour than one finds in Welsch and with a non-Stratian conception of the human sensorium as being heterogenous in form. In this, we take the force of the argument developed in the sixteenth century by Loyola in appealing to all the five the senses of the whole population in encouraging those Catholics, through excitation of their whole sensorium (at different times) to attend Church and thus reject the Reformation because it was so depleted in its sensateness. We hope you will bear with us as we engage in this thought experiment, taking as our focal centre, the practice of architecture. First however, it may be useful to have anaesthetization described for us in graphic form.

Aldous Huxley's *Brave New World* (1932/1994) has within it clear and shocking descriptions of buildings and their functions. Indeed, the book begins with an architectural reference. It establishes the modernity of the future in which it is set by announcing "A squat grey building of only thirty-four storeys" (p. 1). In the *Foreword* of 1946 edition, Huxley presciently sees the great significance of Los Alamos to the post-war world. He says (Huxley, 1946/1994, u.n.):

The most important Manhatten Projects of the future will be vast government-sponsored inquiries into what the politicians and the participating scientists will call 'the problem of happiness'—in other words, the problem of making people love their servitude.

The problem of happiness will be solved, he argues, by better techniques of conditioning, the assignment of human beings into their proper position, a more pleasurable and less harmful drug than gin or heroin through which people may take holidays from reality and a foolproof system of eugenics.

We take this to be an ironic manifesto for anaesthetization.

Below, Huxley describes a conditioning process in which khaki dressed, delta class infants learn to turn away from aesthetic experiences.

the babies at once fell silent, then began to crawl towards those clusters of sleek colours, those shapes so gay and brilliant on the white pages. As they approached, the sun came out of a momentary eclipse behind a cloud. The roses flamed up as though with a sudden passion from within: a new and profound significance seemed to suffuse the shining pages of the books. From the ranks of the crawling babies came little squeals of excitement, gurgles and twitterings of pleasure (Huxley, 1932/1994: 17).

Then "there was a violent explosion. Shriller and ever shriller, a siren shrieked. Alarm bells maddeningly sounded. The children started, screamed: their faces were distorted with terror" (*ibid.*).

'Offer them the flowers and books again'. The nurses obeyed: but at the approach of the roses, at the mere sight of those gaily-colored images of pussy and cock-a-doodle doo and baa-baa black sheep, the infants shrank away in horror (Huxley, 1932/1994: 18).

And whilst, of course, Huxley was describing a world of the future from within the context of the early 1930s there must be a real sense in which the anaesthetizing process within our schools and universities *today* attempts to distort with terror the faces of those exposed to the 'hardships' of reading difficult books and of appreciating the non-human world as if it was of equal significance to the human one. Even Alphas and Alpha pluses within *Brave New World* require regular escapes into an anaethesised existence through the taking of a gramme of stupefying 'soma'.

So what Huxley offers us is a description of a dystopian world in which anaesthetization is literally 'the order of the day'. He sees important connections between the architecture of this dystopian world and its attempts to make people love their servitude. And the culture of the society (based largely on imagery drawn from Fordist America) is one in which most of the aesthetic pleasures of the world cease to be on offer and are replaced by the anodyne anaesthetization of the populace through class based indoctrination and the biochemistry of management.

Clearly, in common understanding, being 'anaetheticised' means no longer being sensate to the world around. It is a form of extreme desensitisation to external and internal stimuli. And this distinction between inner and outer world is important. For are we talking here of the individual's capacity for interest in and ability to seek out the aesthetic being impaired by some form of 'soma'? Or does it mean that the 'anaesthetic' social order does not knowingly provide any aesthetics for the population to enjoy? Is this then an individual or collective issue? Now the reader may see this as a false dichotomy, but the questions asked and answers given depend in large measure on the level of analysis that one begins from. Thus anaesthetics might imply a condition in which beauty could not be appreciated *or* that there was nothing beautiful in the environment to actually appreciate.

Thus the equivalent of an individual, phenomenologically based analysis would produce workers, let us say, who could not appreciate beauty, sought no underlying form or wholeness in what they did, whose senses were dulled and whose higher senses were not developed, whose perceptiveness was dulled by lack of time and whose interest in the external was very low. The materially based equivalent of a social condition such as alienation and the attendant masking of reality would produce a picture of anathesistization as there being nothing beautiful to appreciate, no sense could be made because of the organization of non-integrated parts, which also rendered cosmeticisation futile, that perceptions were artificially lowered by ideological control mechanisms and workers were time starved in order to deprive them of the opportunity to think. In *Brave New World* gammas and epsilons are portrayed as precisely this: anaesthetized drones.

This does not exhaust the range of possibilities, of course, for there is always the possibility that what passes for aesthetics *and* anaesthetics is predicated upon particular class-based power maintaining common understandings of what is meant by the 'cultural'. Does anyone ask the gammas and epsilons what they find beautiful? A rejection of the problematique of aesthetics may be the most constructive way forward for large sections of the population. But nevertheless it is significant to recognise that the aesthetics/anaesthetics dualism does raise many relevant questions for critical management studies.

Elsewhere (Burrell & Dale, in press) we have argued that critical management studies needs to be much more aware of the significance of the built environment and the ways in which management is involved in the building of power, the building of consumption, the building of manufacture and the building of administration. This does not mean that we are interested solely in the buildings of buildings, but rather in the building of the social through buildings. In the present paper, we shall focus on that cultural product known as architecture and ask in what circumstances does the aesthetic/anaesthetic dualism come into play? When do buildings produce an aesthetic experience of the kind Benjamin describes in his *Arcades Project* (*Passagenwerk*, circa 1930s/1999) as *phantasamagoria*? And when do they produce a form of *anaesthesia?*

If anaesthesia, put simply, is about the suppression of the sensate, phantasamagoria are about the excitation of the senses through the surface lustres of beautiful aesthetics used to encourage consumption. The original phantasamagoria in the 19th century were back-lit projections (and, it is important to note, were *not* mere reflections) of ghostly images, onto a screen, that the audience could not detect the provenance thereof. They were bright attractive projections that entertained and amazed audiences. They had and have (for we shall argue that they are still to be found) an aesthetic impact on the crowds for which they were designed. The term becomes generalized in Walter Benjamin's work to mean any deceptive image designed to dazzle (Burrell & Dale, in press).

How then, specifically in the realm of architecture, does Benjamin's notion of phantasamagoria relate to a form of Welsch's anaesthetics? How does the encouragement of a brightly lit *dazzle* square with *desensitisation* of the subject?

First, we must note the emphasis on the visible. The primacy of the visual in the human sensorium is an important part of Benjamin's approach. As Welsch notes, to over-stimulate one part of the sensorium is to under-stimulate the other senses. Thus it is quite easy to see that dazzle and desensitisation can go together in terms of human sensateness. In the presence of bright lights one hears less. But we must note that we are talking here of the single sentient human being. There is more to this than that single point.

Second, it may well be that certain social beings are dazzled and pleased by an aesthetic experience. But at the cost of the desensitisation of those who serve them in the same space. One needs only to consider aesthetic labour (e.g., Hancock & Tyler, 2000) and emotional labour (Hochschild, 1983) to see that the aesthetic experience of flying or entering Disneyfied spaces is at the cost of the self-anaethetised labour of others. Here we are suggesting that one form of anaesthetic used is by staff supposed to engage in emotional labour but who wish to switch off during work (Fineman, 1993; Hochschild, 1983).

Third, the possibility exists that dazzling 'glass-roofed, marble-lined elegance' is a form of aesthetic experience that is predicated in one way or another on the desensitization of those acting at a distance from the lights, those who provide the labour power to achieve the materials for this aesthetic experience. In other words, perhaps the glass factory workers are only offered anaesthetised labour, for sensory deprivation is an integral part of their building and the technological processes that go on within it. And so too of the back-breaking work at the quarry where the marble is hewn.

Fourth, the professionals who aim to produce phantasamagoria (and in this case we refer to architects) must seek to act as dazzlers. However, they are constrained in their art by economics, politics and the power of the client. Only signature architects who engage in Art Architecture may come close to producing beautiful lustres, but for them, some of the time, and for the journeymen and women of the profession, most of the time, compromises have to be made. Professional architects desensitise themselves from not being able to deliver what they want as a full aesthetic experience. Every architect-designed space is, to a greater or lesser extent, a compromise with cost and context in which the aesthetic ideal is lost. Thus architecture is a profession that is anaesthetised, as well as aestheticised, from the outset. Architects cannot seek the full achievement of beauty. Rather, they may have to follow fashion set for them by their clients, who themselves have different and dynamic desires associated with the human sensorium.

Therefore, to dazzle requires desensitisation of the individual who is dazzled, desensitisation of those who labour to produce the dazzle in the same place, desensitisation of those who produce the material to dazzle many miles away and desensitisation of those who produce the designs for the dazzle. Aesthetic labour must also have anaesthetic labour. And this is where, at long last, management comes in. Aesthetics and anaesthetics are both a matter of the *management* of the senses.

When Chester Barnard said in 1939 that management was as much an issue of aesthetics as it was of rationality, he participated in a process of the managerialization of aesthetics. The separation of mind from the senses, of critical reason from practical reason, of sense from sensibility may appear to be a progressive splitting off, for it presents a world in which there are legitimate alternative readings to that derived from reason and rationality. In an issue of the journal *Organization* (1996), on aesthetics and organization, the authors seemed to share a belief that aesthetics offered a parallel interpretation to that derived from managerial rationality and that this should be analysed as an alternative to managerialism. What is amazing, of course, (to us at least) is that the range of human senses supposedly being used in aesthetics—the sensorium—could be seen as remaining untainted by—as independent from—managerial control. The body-in-space is a target for control, discipline, dressage and indoctrination. To assume that it remains a free spirit, outside of the pull of capitalistic rationality, is a triumph of optimism. The interiorization of power flows and the manipulation of the sensorium are totally ignored in much treatment of aesthetics and organization. The current fashion for, and accompanying valorization of, transparent openness in organizational life is reliant upon an obvious manipulation of the human senses and what is to be welcomed by them. The visible is seen (sic) as the valued.

Organizational life, then, is undertaken inside a built environment in which the human body and the sensorium are placed. But we know that the notion that space is empty and is filled by the human physique is not a very social one. It is much better to see the space we inhabit as created by us and by the needs of our enfleshed skeleton. In order to demonstrate this social construction of space, we want to spend a little time discussing an article from

Administrative Science Quarterly (Guillen, 1997) that attempts to widen the debate on Taylorism by suggesting that Taylorism was an aesthetic ideal that spread around the world. We wish to argue that it may well have been an aesthetic for the capitalist classes since it offered to them a wonderful bright *phantasamagoria* of what could be achieved by efficient mass production, but for the labouring classes it represented *anaesthetization* by dulling the senses of those who worked in factories using such principles. The buildings of Albert Kahn, for example, allowed for worker desensitization to the presence of 'zero architecture' inside and outside his factories, factories in which Taylorism and Fordism were to gather apace.

Mauro Guillen (1997) had an article published in *Administrative Science Quarterly* entitled 'Scientific Management's Lost Aesthetic: Architecture, Organization And The Taylorized Beauty Of The Mechanical'. It is worth considering this piece, we would maintain, for it throws into relief the 'an-aesthetic' stance we are to take on the relationship between space, architecture and organization. In many ways it is an exemplary article, sophisticated in its understanding of Europe, historically aware and interested in cultural issues. He seeks to show that the aesthetic 'modernists' in European architecture were highly influenced by Taylorism and saw in it a beauty that latter-day critics, particularly in the social sciences, have not. Guillen (1997) claims that these modernists, such as Gropius, Mies van de Rohe and Le Corbusier, saw in Taylorism and Fordism "beauty with technical, economic and social efficiency" (p. 683). Here, immediately, the reader confronts several problems. Nowhere in the article is aesthetics defined. The level of complexity in defining the term with which we began this paper is totally absent in Guillen. He only looks at 'architects and other artists' who combine 'beauty with technical, economic and social efficiency'. There is, therefore, a certain tendentiousness in the approach that he takes from the outset! He claims that European architects of a modernist persuasion found an aesthetic message in what was going on in the reorganization of production in the USA. Nowhere does Guillen reveal that the European modernists waxed lyrical about the future on what they had seen of Scientific Management's concretization within factory walls, *solely on the basis of a dozen or so grainy photographs*. What he fails to realise is that they seldom visited the USA in this period and much of what they thought they knew was derived from poor quality snapshots. Gropius published North American photos in 1913, but only visited the USA in 1928; Le Corbusier borrowed these images in 1919 and went to the US in 1935 (Banham, 1986: 9). It is very surprising that Guillen does not pick up on this because he certainly references *A Concrete Atlantis* by Reyner Banham (1986) who claims that the work of the European architects in the modernist tradition did copy from American industrial prototypes and models but that: "it must be the first architectural movement in the history of the art based almost exclusively on photographic evidence rather than on the ancient and previously unavoidable techniques of personal inspection and measured drawing" (Banham, 1986: 18).

It is a strange aesthetics, perhaps, that is based on grainy photographs rather than first hand impressions. These aesthetics, we might surmise, were actually in the eye of the (*non*-)beholder. From the distance conveyed through the photographic medium, not only did the European architects not have material knowledge of the design and construction (discussed in Banham, 1986: 18), but they also had no social knowledge of the arrangements and relations of production that actually guided the development of such architectural forms. It was a curiously 'externalist' appropriation that was facilitated by the distancing, singular vision of an optocentric aesthetics. Venturi, Scott-Brown and Izenour (1972: 92-3, discussed in Banham) emphasise that Le Corbusier "claimed the steamship and the grain elevator for their forms rather than their associations, for their simple geometry rather than their industrial lineage". Banham adds that this adoption of the industrial 'style' was symbolic: these buildings appeared to fit the values of the modernist credo with their functional honesty, structural economy and being up to date yet hinting of a futuristic technological utopia.

This abstract and abstracted aesthetics highlights the controversial nature of Guillen's notion that the 'outcomes' of scientific management might not all have been seamy and unpleasant. Clearly if one was an industrialist then this might well be true. Even some scientific managers may have welcomed and embraced the new managerial regimes. Nowhere, however, is the elision between Taylorism, Fordism and Scientific Management confronted. If they were and are separate entities then one has to treat them accordingly. Homogenising them into one category serves little purpose if one wishes to understand their dynamics (Littler, 1985). As with the European modernists, Guillen also seems to be using aesthetics to justify the avoidance of an understanding of the social relations of production.

Elsewhere too, Guillen (1997: 688) seems to find difficulty in the notion that these great architects were only too well aware of the needs of corporate clients. The possession of *avant-garde* credentials does *not* necessarily mean that these talented individuals would take sides against individualistic, mechanistic and engineering based models. After all, these models were sweeping Wilhelmine Germany with their promise of military and industrial success. Why, we might ask, does Guillen find this consanguinity of the avant-garde with capitalism so troubling? It is only to set up the discussion that follows. There is a non-question to which he provides an answer. He is right to say that we have neglected aesthetic issues in Organization Theory but he brings his discussion into being by dissembling about an obvious politico-economic explanation for the motivation of these leading 'Art-Architects'. They sought clients who could and would willingly support their work.

Most importantly, however, the problem of Guillen's focus on the leading figures of architecture, these 'Art-Architects' (Upton, 1998: 262-264), means that he completely ignores the 'journeymen' of the architectural profession who, whilst they do not have artistic pretensions nor abilities, are yet well served by the Art-Architects in the day to day business of making a living. He asserts that things that may be seen as beautiful are aesthetic in some objective sense and therefore the Art-Architects themselves legitimise these forms of cheap industrial building by finding beauty in them. Upton (1998), however, observes that "the conspicuous minority of art-architects bolsters the position of the majority of ordinary practitioners by generating new forms to resupply the professional's visual stock ... imbuing the entire profession with the cultural prestige ... of art" (p. 263).

Thus our argument is that Guillen's piece is to be welcomed for introducing the debate on aesthetics in architecture into the mainstream of organization theory but that it fails to understand the specific differences between particular clients for projects and ultimately opts for a view which privileges that of elite culture and elite capital in its assumptions about aesthetics. From a worker perspective we might hazard a guess that the factories devoted to Taylorism and Fordism, as built according to Kahnism, were places of anaesthetization and zeroes: zero stimulation; zero time for contemplation; zero encouragement of perceptiveness; and, zero architecture. And therefore we turn from the 'externalist' point of view of the aesthetics of modern industrial building, to consider the 'internal' dynamics of the production of these key spaces of twentieth century capitalism.

Born in Germany in 1869, Albert Kahn excelled in the design of buildings for mass production. The construction of single storey buildings covering many acres, illuminated by saw tooth roofs was his trademark. What he developed through his firm was no more and no less than a new paradigm of factory construction. Large factories with their mass production technologies and a workforce used to the rhythms of the industrial day are associated of course with Ford and with Taylor but rarely with Kahn. Yet it is Kahn's development of the 'daylight factory' that produced the spaces in which such efficient mass production work could take place. Beginning with contracts with the Packard Motor Co. in 1903 and thence working for Ford and GM, Kahn established a huge reputation for meeting corporate needs. Most (in)famously, Building Ten of the Packard Motor Company's site in Detroit, is seen by some as a defining moment in 20th century architecture. The building has been described as 'zero architecture' (cf. Banham, 1986: 86).

Culture was thus to disappear into the rapacious cost-sensitive maw of administration. And as this zero-architecture took hold, so too did Kahn take his firm increasingly in the direction of looking more and more like the large firms and state departments with whom he interacted. His huge drawing offices resembled ever more closely the very designs of the buildings upon their drawing boards. One of his contributions then and a key to his success was to develop the large-scale architectural firm that mirrored the large-scale industrial conglomerate. His company grew then by responding to the changes in the US and Soviet economies in the inter-war period and even more so as a result of the Second World War itself. The design principles in his architecture themselves reflected the growth of large-scale bureaucracies. His plans emphasised linearity and hierarchy, with Detroit as the centre of his architectural practice in the same way as it was the centre of medium engineering. Michigan was the gravitational point for his work and it reflected the huge development of the car industry at this time. Also related to this, although not in Kahn's hands, were the public housing programme at Leavittown and the Liberty ship construction programme. Whilst these were and are seen as cheap, low quality and mass-produced architectural activities perhaps these are the very things in which we should be interested. It is not the great figures of architecture in terms of their creative originality of whom we should speak but the utilitarian forces at work which drive forward capital's aims.

The International Style

The intellectual property rights involved in assigning ownership to 'The International Style' are complex and contested. What Guillen has done is to reverse the usually accepted flow of ideas in which architectural aesthetics are seen as running westward. For him, Taylorism moves into Europe in the 1920s as reflective of a new work process in which architects become interested because of its 'elegant' rationalistic forms. For Europeans and most American architects, the lines of influence run the other way in that the USA takes on board the International Style which originates in Europe in the late 1920s. But in the same way as Le Corbusier touched up pictures of Canadian and Argentinian grain silos and called them American, Americans transformed European modernism and air brushed out all the social criticism. Therefore, the Trans-Atlantic flows are indubitably both ways.

In 1931, the year in which *Brave New World* was in the production stage of being published, automobile production in the USA was at about 20% of its 1929 output. Employment in the building industry was less than half of its 1929 level and 85% of all the architects in New York city were out of work (Handlin, 1997: 197). The unemployed looked elsewhere. A new architecture based on a new aesthetic appeared to be developing in Europe. It preached austerity, broke its connections to the older traditions of architecture and made prophetic statements about the new social order based on industrial production. In 1932 an exhibition took place of the 'modern architecture' at the Museum of Modern Art and thereafter this became known as the 'International Style'. According to Hancock and Johnson who organised the exhibition, the new style's aesthetic concerns were with volume not mass (meaning what went into the building was now much more unconstrained), the appearance of a building should reflect its purpose and finally that external decoration served no useful function at all. What this set of principles does, of course, is to strip out any formal discussion of issues of ideology, politics and social relevance. In the European tradition such issues were paramount but once European ideas entered the USA there was a tendency for them to be seen without any sense of context from which they originated. Colin Rowe (quoted in Curtis, 1996: 403) says that "European modern architecture, even when it operated within the cracks and crannies of the capitalist system, existed within an ultimately Socialist ambience. American modern architecture did not". For in America, European architecture "was introduced simply as a new approach to building—and not much more. That is, it was introduced largely purged of its ideological or societal content". Thus, the transformation into some neutered form of those *avant garde* political aspirations for and of art-architecture, took place very easily indeed within the USA. Housing, for example, was given a very low status in the USA's appropriation of the International Style and whilst the Tennessee Valley Authority (studied by Selznick in 1947 as one of the classic pieces of organisational analysis) did represent Government-sponsored attempts to raise the profile of such social planning, it failed dismally to achieve this objective.

Somewhat perplexingly, Kahn despised the International Style when he may well have been seen as engaging in precisely the same sort of aesthetic. But he saw it as the lowest form of architecture. Architecture in its proper sense was about ceremonial purpose. Functionality (in which most of his practice specialised) was the least important in the hierarchy of the discipline. Of Gropius's work he asked "Is it architecture at all?" and that of Le Corbusier was "utterly stupid" (Handlin, 1997: 209). This is why he could be sanguine about his own buildings being 'zero architecture' for he saw such a condition all around him in the new European style. It was not proper architecture. This stance came from a visit he made in 1881 to various European cities, with Henry Bacon, a colleague, who was later to design the Lincoln Memorial. They were both influenced by the classicism of the Beaux Arts movement in France and thereafter saw 'real' buildings as being necessarily monumental, with a clear architectural hierarchy existing from ceremonial buildings at the top and functional buildings way down at the bottom.

Harvey Wiley Corbett (1873-1954) argued that "advertising, exploitation and publicity were the animating agents behind the commercial age" (1924, quoted in Handlin, 1997: 183). The architect, according to Corbett, had to give expression to these forces and the skyscraper, the architectural form with which he is associated, must have a distinct physiognomy which would really identify the company who paid for it to be built. Skidmore Owings and Merrill (SOM) were just such a company who were able and willing to provide corporate identity through monumental buildings. Influenced by Ludwig Mies van de Rohe (1886-1969) with his image of the tall building by which to set agendas, they opened their office in Chicago in 1936 but immediately also placed themselves in New York.

Thus SOM were the heirs to Kahn's 'utilitarian boxes'; they were the firm who took this aesthetic of function and fully stripped out any sense of left wing confrontation within it. Beginning with their successful bid to the US Army for the design for the facilities of the Manhattan Project at Los Alamos (and their ultra sensitivity to reflecting military hierarchy that this necessitated), SOM went on to develop their version of the International Style into the house style of corporate capitalism. Office buildings became great phantasamagoria in the sky. They were phallic symbols of the potency of their Chief Executive Officers and, through their glass curtain walls, spoke to the audiences, paraded before them in the streets of the metropolitan centres, of their brightness and powers of illumination made possible by their amassed dollars. The appeal to corporate owners comes from their phantasmagoric capabilities to dazzle. These office blocks conventionally represented 'sky-scrapers' but offered more symbolically, penetration of the clouds. Yet, as within the factories of Kahn, they relied upon anesthetized bureaucrats labouring within. The buildings of SOM which came to dominate office building in the latter half of the 20th century were also places of anaesthetics and zeroes.

But, of course, it would be foolish to think that politics had been stripped out of the International Style completely. SOM reflected a politics which was anti-union, anti-'liberal' and anti-craft ethic (one of the ways in which they achieved these goals was the widespread use of mass produced, prefabricated components, factory-built and then shipped to the site—a commonplace activity now but initially a radical move). The aesthetics of Hancock and Johnson were supposedly outside of politics but what this masked was the capture of left leaning socially aware architecture by American corporate architects whose politics, were they to win business for their offices, had to be inclined to the right.

So, in America or elsewhere is it possible even to envisage architectures that do not anaesthetise and that do not represent a phantasamagorian dazzle designed to simultaneously desensitise?

Architectures of Emancipation?

Rather than a rationalist view of the aesthetics of architecture which posits that the structure and form of a building reflects its functions, and that these functions are hierarchically arranged—with of course the architecture of industry at the bottom—we have sought to argue a more complex relationship between aesthetics and organisation. Art has often been seen as somehow autonomous from the social and political relations in which it has been produced. Through this relative autonomy it could stand outside and protest against the 'petrified relations' of bourgeois society. Theodor Adorno was keen to assert in his aesthetic theory that art had an emancipatory potential, through its presenting of a vision of an alternative world. Art which required the engagement of the observer and was not merely an entertainment or distraction had this potential to liberate (Leach, 1997: 17-19).

Following Adorno, who here prefigures much of what Welsch has to say in his tour of the meanings of aesthetics, Architecture as Art may be assumed to be where every detail/part is central to the totality of the enterprise; themes and detail are highly interwoven and the latter cannot be changed without affecting the whole; a high level of technical competence is required. The audience for the building or edifice which is high art have to experience all of it, they have to concentrate on it very hard for it is like no other piece and ultimately it is disruptive of the continuum of everyday life (cf. Held, 1980: 101, 103). Architecture devoid of art (in a sense 'zero architecture') reflects the opposite tendencies. The piece uses familiar and cliched frameworks; it is repetitive, rigid and underdeveloped thematically. Stress is on individual effects not the totality and therefore detail can be substituted at will. The conventional norms are unchallengingly supported by such edifices. Audiences react to such artless buildings by responding to the parts not the whole. The piece is standardised and already known and predictable; little effort is required to understand it and there is manipulation of the form and content so that they appear familiar. This sense of pre-existing recognition produces pleasure for the observer and the quality of the building is measured by how often it is repeated. Thus it reinforces a sense of continuity with everyday life and renders the process of thinking unnecessary.

The problem with such an analysis is that one cannot assume that difficult and disruptive buildings which challenge the status quo are necessarily going to rely on an aesthetics which are sympathetic to the workforce! Surely it might be possible for aesthetically challenging edifices to be erected which are antagonistic to subordinate value systems and quality of life.

Adorno thought that 'authentic art' would succumb to 'the culture industry' where its consumers, the workforce, were at their weakest and most ill-informed. He saw Benjamin as having embraced " the anarchistic romanticism of blind confidence in the spontaneous power of the proletariat" (quoted in Held, 1980: 88) and instead of this he advocated the merits of work which both rejects market requirements and nineteenth century philosophies and embraces the dissonant character of the twentieth century. For him, that authentic art which was revolutionary in a Left wing sense was likely to be under real threat. What he did not fully address was art which is revolutionary in a right wing sense. However, Adorno did recognise that the inaccessibility of high art would reduce its revolutionary effectiveness for the Left. The relationship between architecture, aesthetics and high art on one hand and the power of the workforce, spontaneous or not, on the other, therefore does merit further investigation and is more complex than Adorno recognised. High culture in the form of Art Architecture can be authentically autonomous from what has gone before but nevertheless culturally emiserate large sections of the populace. Indeed, revolutionary new buildings derived from the domain of Art Architects can be just like the buildings of popular culture: profoundly enslaving.

So, in concluding this paper, we seek not to find and analyse architecture which is only left-leaning high art on one hand or an architecture of popular culture which reinforces the existing structures of domination on the other. Rather, for us, architecture is a practice which can be conceptualised as being other things. First, it might be revolutionary from the point of view of the interests of Capital and with aesthetic content from the phenomenological standpoint of the organizational subordinate. Bel Geddes' design for the General Motors stand 'Futurama', in 1939, seems to have some of these features. In what prefigures a lot of Disney type rides, visitors (sometimes GM car workers) were placed in a travelling vehicle from which they were meant to see the freeways of 1960 and the ameliorating effects these was to have on city life. By all accounts, visitors were amazed and delighted by this diarama. It can be seen as a phantasamagoria which dazzled the consumer and allowed GM to press ahead for freeway expansion on a massive scale. But it moved almost all who saw it. Second, architecture is possible which is revolutionary in the interests of Capital without aesthetic interest from the viewpoint of the subordinate. The interpretation of the subordinate is important but it may well be that he/she sees an architectural aesthetic (or not) because of manipulation of their sensorium. This is the sort of position we think that Huxley is adopting in *Brave New World.* Most crucially, however, for us is that third case where an architecture may be devoid of aesthetic intentions or interpretations on the parts of the architect, perhaps even the client and certainly their subordinates, yet it may be truly revolutionary. It may be the architectural soma which induces anaesthetization. This description perhaps is what fits the factory design work of Albert Kahn.

One final contemporary example may serve to bring these themes up-to-date. This is the headquarters building of PowerGen, constructed in the mid-1990s and receiving a number of awards for its innovation. Despite this we are not selecting it because of its uniqueness but its typification of the an-aesthetics in organizational aesthetics. The building is constructed as one large space, around an atrium at its centre which allows all three floors to be observed at a glance. However, the effect of such a large space on the senses is surprisingly deadened. The noise levels of up to 600 workers in this open space would be expected to be deafening, but the sound is flattened through the pumping of 'white-noise' which removes the highs and the lows upon the ear of the listener. The atmosphere is also constant and consistent—kept so by a computerised building management system. Visually, the experience of the architecture is one of levelling, transparency and consistency: there are few contrasts or surprises, and a lack of variation in color and texture. The overall impression, then, is one of calm control of the environment: a fitting setting for professional bureaucratized man and woman?

Conclusion

Saskia Sassen (2000: 168-9) has argued that: "the emphasis on hypermobility, global communications and the neutralization of place and distance needs to be balanced with a focus on the *work* behind command functions, on the actual *production process* in the leading information industries, finance and specialised services and on global market*places*" (italics in original). In this paper we have tried to take these notions of material conditions, sites of production and place boundedness very seriously indeed.

Harry Braverman (1974), a figure whose influence on our subject has been enormous, in his discussion of the Labour Process writes almost nothing on space and place. Whilst it is clear that he did discuss the importance of production processes and was incisive about the materiality of this process, in his sections about Taylorism and Human Relations, about factory and office, these notions are 'deterritorialized' so that they appear to be universal and placeless. What we have sought to argue is that architecture played a key role in the 20th century's development of management practice and the labour process and that our understandings of space and the place of the human body within it are highly influenced by our architectural confinements. Following Merleau-Ponty, Harvey and more importantly Henri Lefebvre, however, the space we inhabit with our bodies is not to be seen as abstract space, nor is it formal space. It is lived space and has to be seen phenomenologically. We are not looking here for space for the body but at the-body-in-space. Human interpretations of the significance of this lived space must be placed at the forefront of our analysis rather than being conveniently forgotten.

In seeking to portray the body-in-space from more of a phenomenological perspective, our encounter with aesthetics raises several issues. Is the desire to find an independent aesthetics across the full range of the human sensorium capable of being fulfilled? And is the search for authentic architecture capable of being realised? Or, is aesthetics merely a hand-maiden of management? And, is any piece of authentic art able to withstand this pressure to accommodate and comply?

Sassen's encouragement in the face of acres of 'virtuality' to remember material conditions, production sites and place boundedness struck us as important. Office blocks and factories have an ontological depth which confronts the phenomenological world of the body-in-space. We have not space here to explore the philosophical implications of the architecture we inhabit. The opening offered here is one centred on placed, material, sites of production. Frampton (1992) has argued that 'Productivism' is a dominant force in architecture. The central tenet of this style is that architecture is nothing more than elegant engineering and is the product of industrial design on a gigantic scale. The task should be accommodated as far as possible in an undecorated shed that should be as flexible and as open as possible. Openness and flexibility are best served by the services to and within the building being treated in an integrated way and finally the building itself should represent the unimpeded manifestation of production. In their own ways and in different halves of the twentieth century the designs of Kahn and of SOM represent forms of productivism. These two companies have produced buildings all around the world which are cheap to construct, are destructive of craft skills, comfortably meet the symbolic and material needs of capital, and, in their different ways, build upon anaesthetics more than aesthetics. Their success depends also on their incorporation into the dominant social institutions and norms of their time. Thus we emphasise the significance of the everyday architect and architectural practices, and their relationship with business. However, it is perhaps not the architects, great or otherwise, nor the capitalist class that we should focus on but the effects on our very *selves* of the anaesthetics and the aesthetics of our built environment. It is important that issues of space, building and design, very often taken-for-granted in our experience of everyday life, are incorporated into our understanding of alienation and identity.

A critical management studies must be critical, first and foremost, of its own production and consumption of knowledge. Thus, in our discussions of aesthetics and organisation, we must be careful not to de-politicise the nature of the material, embodied relations of production of which we write, in favour of more romanticised, beautiful—but, perhaps anaestheticising—versions of organisational life.

References

Adorno, T. (2001). *The culture industry* (J. Bernstein, Ed.). London: Routledge. (Original work published 1991).

Banham, R. (1986). *A concrete Atlantis.* Cambridge, MA: MIT.

Barnard, C. (1939). *Functions of the executive.* Cambridge, MA: Harvard University.

Benjamin, W. (1999). *The arcades project* (K. McLaughlin & H. Eiland, Trans.). Cambridge, MA: Belknap/Harvard University. (Original work written circa 1930s).

Braverman, H. (1974). *Labour and monopoly capital.* London: Monthly Review.

Burrell, G., & Dale, K. (in press). Building better worlds? Architecture, space and organisation. In M. Alvesson & H. Willmott (Eds.), *Critical management studies* (2nd ed.). London: Sage.

Curtis, W. (1996). *Modern architecture since 1900.* London: Phaidon.

Fineman, S. (Ed.). (1993). *Emotions and organisation.* London: Sage.

Frampton, K. (1992). *Modern architecture: A critical history.* London: Thames and Hudson.

Guillen, M. (1997). Scientific management's lost aesthetic: Architecture, organization and the Taylorised beauty of the mechanical. *Administrative Science Quarterly, 42*, 682-715.

Hancock, P., & Tyler, M. (2000). 'The look of love': Gender and the organization of aesthetics. In J. Hassard, R. Holliday &

H. Willmott (Eds.), *Body and organization* (pp. 108-129). London: Sage.

Handlin, D. (1997). *American architecture.* London: Thames and Hudson.

Held, D. (1980). *Introduction to critical theory.* Oxford: Polity.

Hochschild, A. (1983). *The managed heart.* Berkeley, CA: University of California.

Huxley, A. (1994). *Brave new world.* London: Chatto and Windus. (Original work published 1932).

Huxley, A. (1994). Foreword. In A. Huxley, *Brave new world (Rev. Foreword ed. u.n.).* London: Chatto and Windus. (Original foreword revised 1946).

Leach, D. (Ed.). (1997). *Architecture and philosophy.* London: Routledge.

Littler, C. (1982). *The development of the labour process in capitalist societies.* London: Heinemann.

Marx, K. (1972). *The Marx-Engels reader* (R. Tucker, Ed.). New York: Norton. (Original work published 1844).

Organization, (1996). Special section on Aesthetics and organization, 3, 189-248.

Sassen, S. (2000). Excavating power. *Theory Culture and Society,* 17, 163-170.

Selznick, P. (1949). *TVA and the grassroots.* Berkeley, CA: University of California.

Strati, A. (1999). *Organization and aesthetics.* London: Sage.

Upton, D. (1998). *Architecture in the United States.* Oxford: OUP.

Venturi, R., Scott-Brown, D., & Izenour, S. (1972). *Learning from Las Vegas.* Cambridge, MA: Cambridge.

Welsch, W. (1997). *Undoing aesthetics.* London: Sage.

Chapter 6
Aestheticizing the World of Organization: Creating Beautiful Untrue Things

Philip Hancock

The final revelation is that lying, the telling of beautiful untrue things, is the proper aim of art. Oscar Wilde—The Decay of Lying (1905/1913: 54)

Introduction

The aesthetic has long endured an uneasy relationship with institutions of power and authority. For Plato (trans. 1955/1987), the subversive potential he detected in the practice of art, and the aesthetic it engendered, was sufficient for him to call for poets and performers to be banned from his ideal Republic, lest they should corrupt his guardians and future philosopher kings. For the great minds of the Enlightenment the aesthetic, something unwieldy and corporeal in its nature, threatened their idealized realm of mind and led Kant (1790/1952) to construct his elaborate philosophical system to ensure its subservience to the exercise of reason and judgement. More recently, the 19th and the 20th centuries saw a great explosion in both the emergence of art and aesthetic practice as a force of political and cultural radicalism, yet while at the same time it increasingly became the preserve of the rich and powerful to accumulate and enjoy.

Today, however, in these so-called postmodern times, it would seem that the aesthetic has finally been liberated. Freed by the democratizing forces of market capitalism and no longer formally restricted to the domain of art, aestheticized experience is available everywhere and to everyone: in the local high street, through the media and even, in the workplace. We consume on the basis of style, symbolism and fashion. Our bodies have become aesthetic projects to be adorned, toned and displayed. Even the organizations we work for are now, or so it would seem, getting in on this particular act. Not only is the value of corporate art collections on the increase (see Jacobson, 1993, 1996), but, in the wake of the corporate culture movement (Deal & Kennedy, 1982) and calls for more managed emotion in the workplace (Cooper & Sawaf, 1998), it would now seem that organizations are themselves becoming increasingly sensitive to aesthetic values. In the UK the mainstream business press have, for example, started to run stories and articles on the recognized importance of aesthetics to 'efficient' office design (Gardner, 2001) and the role artistic activities can play in motivating and retaining staff (Pollock, 2000). Radio and television programmes have discussed issues ranging from the impact of the aesthetics of PowerPoint presentations on organizational thinking, to the aesthetic of organized religion and how big business can and should learn from it. Furthermore, this is not simply an organizational issue in the narrow sense of the term. From designer outlets to glossy and stylized public relations documents, vehicle livery to the training of staff in self-presentation, corporate organizations are also increasingly playing a major role in the landscaping of our everyday aesthetic environment. Issues of organizational aesthetics are also therefore, increasingly socio-cultural issues as the modern distinction between formal organization and culture is rendered increasingly meaningless.

So how are critical theorists of organization and society to interpret such developments? Do they take them to represent a possible desublimation of the sensuality of society, or rather, should they look upon them as yet a further example of the ever-encroaching tide of rationalization that continues to haunt and undermine the emancipatory vision of critical social theory? In this chapter, what I seek to do is approach such questions through the critical textual scrutiny of some of the work that has recently emerged to champion such developments, particularly that which exults organizational managers to take seriously the need to make strategic interventions into the realm of organizational aesthetics. In doing so, and drawing on a range of theoretical resources including those to be found in the work of Theodor Adorno, Stjepan Mestrovic and Wolfgang Welsch, I then attempt to draw some critical conclusions regarding what I argue here is a process of organizational aestheticization, maintaining that rather than representing the emancipation of the aesthetic, such developments can be more accurately understood to represent the potential negation of the unique, and possibly emancipatory qualities of the aesthetic as a realm of non-conceptual experience.

The Problem of Everyday Aestheticization

We are, as Wolfgang Welsch (1997: 1) has noted, "without doubt currently experiencing an aesthetics boom". While a multi-faceted process, integral to this "boom" is what he refers to as a process of surface aestheticization—the embellishment and sensualization of everyday objects, environments and experiences. Yet despite the initial impressions (sic), the term surface may give, we should not necessarily take it to imply something trivial or inconsequential. For to refer to the surface in this context is to refer, I would suggest, to the conceptual and physical space within which our everyday experiences and understandings of the world around us are negotiated and reproduced. That is, a constantly contested space within which human subjects are able to exercise their potential for subjective understanding and inter-subjective communication based on the autonomous realization of will, and the practice of undistorted communication (Habermas, 1981/1984). Yet, as the term "contested" suggests, this everyday realm is one within which a multitude of forces and interests play themselves out, each both potentially threatening and facilitating the possibility of human relations based on the values and practice of autonomy, creativity and respect.

The potential aestheticization of this everyday space has, perhaps not surprisingly therefore, encountered somewhat mixed reactions. For Featherstone (1991), for example, this aestheticization of the mundane is taken as the positive outcome of a consumer culture that actually promotes the asetheticization of the rational and instrumental components of consumer capitalism. Thus, sociocultural aestheticization is taken to represent a celebration of human creativity in a world of people who "have a sense of adventure and take risks to explore life's options to the full, who are conscious they have only one life to live and must work hard to enjoy, experience and express it" (p. 59). Posited against such optimism, however, sits an alternative perspective, one more critical and wary of the origins, and potential implications, of such an aestheticization process. Drawing in particular on the legacy of the Critical Theory of the Frankfurt School in general, and the work of Adorno, Horkheimer and Marcuse in particular, it challenges the relationship outlined above between aestheticization and rationality in that it considers it to be a rationalization and instrumentalization of the aesthetic that in fact underpins such developments. A process that, in turn, rather than valorizing the aesthetic dimension of everyday life, signifies the negation of aesthetic experience as a unique and potentially emancipatory mode of apprehending the world.

Yet while normatively and politically divergent, what evidently unites these perspectives is a shared awareness of the economic basis of such a process. Now of course, for Featherstone, while proving a useful starting point for his theorization, ultimately the primacy of economic analysis is rendered somewhat obsolete by what he considers to be the elevated prominence of cultural determinism within contemporary societies. However, for the more Marxist inspired tradition of Critical Theory it is the economic dimension that provides, in large part, the basis for its critique of what is considered to be the debasement of western art and culture by the reductionist and instrumentalist logic of commodity capitalism (Adorno & Horkheimer, 1944/1979). This assault on the value of aesthetic experience is viewed, therefore, as essentially a colonization process whereby, as Welsch (1997: 3) notes, aesthetic values can even be employed to rehabilitate and promote, for instance, commodities that have otherwise become "increasingly unusable on moral or health grounds". The main concern here then is not simply that contemporary aestheticization processes render us increasingly vulnerable to the practices of advertisers and marketeers. Rather, as I have intimated above, what may also be at stake is the quality of the aesthetic as an integral aspect of human culture and experience, facing as it does the onslaught of a rationalization process that reduces it to little more than yet another quantifiable variable, devoid not only of the magical quality of sensuality, but that emancipatory potential which, as Marcuse (1978/1979: 69) notes, has for so long deferred its promise of "freedom and happiness for the individual".

What is particularly interesting in the context of this collection, however, is that for those concerned with developing a critical approach to the ideas and practices underpinning contemporary organizational activity, such debates are also coming to take on a newly invigorated importance. For organizations, as Berg and Kreiner (1990) observed over a decade ago, have been no less seduced by the aestheticization processes apparently availing the rest of society resulting, in turn, in the emergence of a sizeable body of literature both extolling, and warily acknowledging, the implications of aesthetics for the contemporary organizational endeavour. In relation to this latter genre, along with Strati's (1990, 1992, 1996, 1999, 2000a, 2000b) sizeable contribution to the development of an aesthetically driven approach to organization studies itself, several authors have subsequently addressed what they consider to be a range of negative manifestations of the purposeful manipulation and management of aesthetics within the organizational domain. Drawing on Gagliardi's (1990, 1996) re-formulation of the aesthetic capacity of the organizational artifact, for example, Larsen and Schultz's (1990) study of a Danish bureaucracy addresses the ways in which material artifacts ranging from office furnishings to the physical posturing of individual bodies, can be manipulated to maintain the perceived legitimacy of asymmetrical organizational power relations, and thus function as pervasive technologies of unconscious control.

Other examples of this more critical approach to the aestheticization of organizational life can also be found in recent work, such as that by Hancock and Tyler (2000), Höpfl (2000), and Thompson, Warhurst and Callaghan (2000), all of whom have focused on how the management of both environmental and embodied aesthetics can be understood to operate as a mechanism of employee control through what Witkin (1990: 332) has referred to as the "positive cultivation of certain sensuous values that directly express or realize the organizational presence demanded". However, as the work of Carter and Jackson (2000) suggests, the capacity for organizational aesthetics to influence and cultivate the sensuous is not necessarily restricted to the interior of the organizational domain. As their study of the work of the Commonwealth War Graves Commission illustrates, the aestheticization of organizational activities can serve an important function in terms of reinforcing far wider socio-cultural belief systems. For while the formal role of the Commission is the "care and maintenance of cemeteries and memorials for military war dead" (Carter & Jackson, 2000: 184), underpinning this responsibility, they argue, is the material generation of an aesthetic designed to invoke, through the orderly and dignified design of such facilities, a "feeling of solace and peace and not of depression" (Gibson & Ward, cited in Carter & Jackson, 2000: 184). While at first sight this could be taken to represent simply an attempt to generate an appropriate sense of dignity and respect for the deceased, the account put forward by the authors is somewhat more critical, and perhaps rather more insightful. For by locating the interpretation of such physical spaces within the context of a broader critical theory of the relationship between authority and the portrayal of war, they somewhat convincingly suggest that what they actually represent are aesthetically engineered spaces designed to deny their relationship to the experience of war, death, destruction and chaos. Of equal importance, however, is that in doing so they also actively favour the values of universal order and reason that, in turn, obscures both the irrationality of modern warfare and the irrationality of a social and political order which so often perpetrates or justifies such acts of destruction.

Organizational aesthetics, in this instance at least, can therefore be said to transcend the particular realm of the organization itself, and function to reinforce the more general cultural regime characteristic of modernity and its unapologetic adherence to the formality of post-enlightenment rationality; whatever the human cost incurred. Yet as I noted earlier, not all literature is so critically inclined. While the imperative in the material I have considered above is the identification and critique of a process of instrumental appropriation directed towards the aesthetic dimension of experience, an alternative body of literature has also recently emerged which presents itself in very different terms. For in contrast to say the work of Carter and Jackson, its authors consider the organizational appropriation, and manipulation, of the aesthetic dimension to be not only a positive development in traditional business terms, but also to offer a potentially liberating experience for society as a whole. Such material, therefore, extols the virtue of the aesthetic and its capacity to both stimulate organizational competitiveness and efficiency while, at one and the same time, fostering the capacity of contemporary work organizations to enhance the quality of the aesthetic experience of society as a whole.

Yet despite such apparently noble intent, what I propose in the remainder of this paper, and drawing on the critical tradition alluded to above, is that such literature in fact does little more than to further reduce the reduction of the aesthetic to the status of an instrumentalized carrier of a very particular organizational ideology. Furthermore, to achieve this, it would seem that even despite the literatures acknowledgement of the uniqueness of the aesthetic as a mode of commercial, if not social engagement, it must still be stripped of its intangible or ineffable qualities, as well as any notion of experiential autonomy, reducing it to the level of yet another a quantifiable variable within the design of a broader organizational system. As such, the aesthetic as a critical mode of experience and cognition is itself emasculated, reduced to the status of yet another heteronymous ordered component within the organized environment of contemporary consumer capitalism—and like Carter and Jackson's cemeteries—left to function as an engineered legitimation of the dominance of an instrumentalized and dehumanized culture.

Designing the Beautiful Organization

Before proceeding any further, it is perhaps worth stating one important caveat, namely, that in no way should it be taken that I am suggesting that an instrumental attitude towards the aesthetic and its relationship to the pursuit of commercial gain or organizational productivity is, in itself, entirely novel. From the requirement for aesthetic labour, to the use of designers, architects and artists to generate brand or corporate identities, the relationship between them is as old, if not far older, than capitalism itself. For example, architecture, as Olins (1989) observes referring to the great London railway stations built during the 19th century and, more latterly, the imposing City headquarters of the Midland Bank which, when it was built in 1924, was the wealthiest such institution in the world, provides a striking illustration of this fact. Today, the felt need to express one's corporate power and position through the design and scale of one's public buildings is no less diminished of course. Structures such as the Chrysler Building in New York, the Bank of China tower in Hong Kong, or the recently completed Citigroup Building on London's' Canary Wharf function not simply as containers, but as Berg and Kreiner (1990: 43) would have it, "impelling symbols of corporate virtues and managerial intentions". However, what is perhaps increasingly significant today is the potential for organizations to generate, project and sustain an aestheticized relationship between themselves and their increasingly diverse range of stakeholders via a far greater range of media than simply buildings and product advertising. Now while in part this is a consequence of technological developments and the increased primacy of information and knowledge management within society as a whole, what is also significant is the requirement for organizations to able to communicate a commercially attractive and publicly memorable identity, largely in response to the pressures of intensified global competition, at each and every opportunity that presents itself. Thus, from product advertisements to annual reports, internal newsletters to recruitment brochures and mission statements to web sites, increasingly the emphasis is being placed on taking the opportunity to "get across the right image", "look good" and "make a strong impression" in order to maintain or achieve even the slightest of market advantages.

Yet it is not so much the quantitative increase in the amount of aestheticized material being produced by contemporary organizations that is of primary concern here, but rather the qualitative shift this may have generated in terms of how the category of the aesthetic is experienced within contemporary organizational circles and society at large. What I am suggesting by this, is not simply that aesthetic experience is increasingly coming to serve the economic interests of the corporate sphere—a somewhat inevitable process—but the idea that in doing so, it is in fact becoming identical with, or reduced to it. By this I mean that we are facing a potential situation whereby aesthetic experience no longer simply serves the requirements of the corporate sphere, but where corporate style and beauty becomes style and beauty per se, and aesthetic experience is valued at naught unless it is formally sanctioned though organizational affiliation or corporate association: a world where the sanitized, plastic beauty of organizational aesthetics provides the only credible, or indeed legitimate, source of aesthetic gratification.

Certainly, there are others who share a concern that such a shift in our cultural sensibilities may already be taking place. As I indicated earlier Welsch (1997: 3), for example, notes how it is evident that the ongoing surface aestheticization of contemporary western societies is, in large part, driven by the increasingly aestheticized nature of marketable commodities. This is occurring, he goes on to argue, and clearly drawing on the work of Baudrillard (1981), to the extent whereby even the exchange value of commodities is supplanted by their "aesthetic aura" which itself becomes the consumer's "primary acquisition, with the article merely incidental". Equally, in her polemical account of the continuing expansion of the corporate brand into almost every facet of our everyday lives, Klein (1999/2001) provides a not dissimilar set of observations. For instance, she notes how it is becoming not merely accepted, but culturally expected that major leisure and arts events should be accompanied by sponsorship relations that ensure that every aspect of the experience is stamped and adorned with the aestheticized identity of the sponsor themselves. Thus, every kind of aesthetic event, from popular music tours, to art exhibitions, television drama and theatrical productions are, in Klein's view, on the verge of becoming indistinguishable from the aestheticized experience of the corporate sponsorship upon which such events now rely. Perhaps more telling, however, is the work I referred to nearer the beginning of this paper, that which is directly concerned with promoting the systematic process of organizational aestheticization and the benefits it can bring, and to which I now want to turn my attentions.

It is in the work of Bernd Schmitt and what he terms his Corporate Aesthetics Management (CAM) Framework that the drive to establish a systematic approach to the planning and design of an aestheticized organizational environment is probably best exemplified. Schmitt, author of a number of single-authored and collaborative works (Schmitt, 2000; Schmitt, Simonson & Marcus, 1995; Schmitt & Simonson, 1997), first outlined his strategic approach to management of organizational aesthetics in a journal article entitled *Managing Corporate Image and Identity* (Schmitt, Simonson & Marcus, 1995). While he acknowledges that, generally speaking, organizational managers have tended to sidestep discussions on aesthetics due to the somewhat esoteric and generally subjective nature of the topic, for Schmitt the solution to this 'problem' is simply to reduce the language of the aesthetic to a style (sic) more 'familiar' to managers, thus allowing it to be more easily comprehended and deployed as the basis for a "comprehensive and strategic approach...to [managing] a corporations aesthetic image" (Schmitt *et al.*, 1995: 83).

The path that Schmitt and his colleagues take in this respect commences, perhaps not surprisingly, with the act of definition. That is, by defining the object of their attentions, namely *corporate aesthetics*, they are able provide a readily digestible reduction of a complex concept while, at the same time, establishing important socially grounded relations as somehow natural or almost inevitable such as the very conjunction of the two terms or the relationship between corporate imagery and the possibility of "gratification",

> *...the term 'corporate aesthetics' is used in its broadest sense to refer to a company's visual (and otherwise aesthetic) output in the form of packaging, logos, trade names, business cards, company uniforms, buildings, advertisements and other corporate elements that have the potential of providing aesthetic gratification* (Schmitt *et al.*, 1995: 83).

The focus of their strategy, it should also be noted, is then placed firmly on the evaluation of material artifacts as the aesthetic components of the organization. Thus, the subjective dimension of aesthetic experience is, or so it appears, carefully excluded, further reducing potential obstacles to the construction of a systematic framework within which the aesthetic may be reduced to a series of variables, subject to manipulation over both time and space.

Thus having now reduced the aesthetic to a discursively knowable and materially quantifiable entity, it is then possible to 'slot' it into the CAM framework and articulate the necessary categorizations, procedures and assessment criteria which, we are informed, provide an approach to the management of aesthetics that is "systematic", "comprehensive" and "strategic" (Schmitt *et al.*, 1995: 83). So, like the architectural projects associated with high modernism, for example, aesthetic concerns are determined by the principles of order, calculability and replicability that already underpin the organizational logic familiar to individuals like Schmitt. Its own aesthetic is that of the machine, which then almost inevitably descends into the formulaic management-speak of systems, sub-systems and strategies as managers are counselled in the need to undertake careful and systematic analyses, calculations and evaluations as part of their aesthetics management strategies. Take, for example, the following passage describing the structure of an aesthetics situation analysis,

The situation analysis encompasses four distinct sub-stages, each reflecting a separate goal (see Figure 2.). The first sub-stage consists of a thorough status quo analysis of every aspect of a company's image. Without proper identification of all image-related elements, the comprehensive, systematic and strategic qualities are compromised (Schmitt *et al.*, 1995: 84).

Notably, a central component of this situation analysis are what the authors describe as the four "P categories" of aesthetics management, "properties, products, presentations and publications", all of which must be carefully evaluated (although we are warned that the initial sub-divisions may require the use of "subjective judgements") to ensure a sound knowledge base is provided with regard to the aesthetics of the existing corporate image. Further stages then follow; the design of a corporate aesthetics strategy, the building of design elements, and finally a process for aesthetic quality control through which consistency of image and style may be maintained and necessary updates and upgrades undertaken.

In the more substantial text, *Marketing Aesthetics* (Schmitt & Simonson, 1997), not only is the CAM framework refined, but the emphasis shifts to the presentation of a fully blown "self-help" or "how to" manual for budding aesthetics managers. Here, everything from style to various architectural and geometric forms is identified, defined and then illustrated in their specific application. Perhaps more significant, however, are the examples the authors provide of what they consider to be particularly successful attempts at generating very specific aestheticized identities by several leading companies. Starbucks, IBM and GAP all provide case studies of organizations whose approach to the management of aesthetics has led the way in the use of images, sounds, smells and textures as tools to achieve "tangible value for the organization" (Schmitt & Simonson, 1997: 21) including "increased consumer loyalty, the ability to charge higher prices for similar products and increased employee productivity". So while such organizations increasingly contribute to the aesthetic landscape of contemporary western culture, the aesthetic is itself, or so it would seem, contemporaneously reduced to an equivalent value, one identical to the value such organizations place upon it as a resource for the maximization of profit and the marginalization of potential competition.

Now it has to be admitted that in many respects the work of Schmitt and his colleagues offers something of an obvious target for the kind of criticism I have presented above. For despite their allusions to the generation of cultural value and the like, they do not, after all, entirely shy away from articulating the priorities underpinning their efforts, namely to ensure corporate leaders recognize the aesthetic dimension as a potential resource, which, as with any other resource, exists to be exploited. As such, the aesthetic, as the realm of sensory apprehension, is clearly conceptualized and articulated as a site of strategic managerial intervention, amenable to qualification and quantification, analysis, appropriation and finally, purposeful commodification, while the potential wider consequences of this are not, at the end of the day, overly concerning to them. However, the same cannot be so straightforwardly said of the work of Dickinson and Svensen (2000), whose *Beautiful Corporations: Corporate Style in Action* signifies a very different approach to the issue at hand.

Unlike Schmitt and Simonson's offering, this appears to be no work of sensible scientism and fathomable frameworks. Indeed, one's very first encounter with this particular artifact is itself—like an increasing number of new-wave management texts—profoundly material and aestheticized. The dust cover, striking in design, verges on the fluorescent. The inside combines paper that is silky to the touch with full-page glossy photos and engaging montages while the text is organized in short, punchy paragraphs laid out with plenty of space to spare and punctuated with 'stylish' images and MTVesque soundbites. Certainly more corporate coffee table than corporate boardroom, more pop culture than intellectual treatise, its aesthetic is one of fun, accessibility, and the feeling that business can be cool, slick and stylish. Even when one ventures beyond (or below) this level of engagement, the narrative is apparently equally different in content to Schmitt and Simonson's. Rather than a technical manual, this is a direct evocation to a more attractive world through organizational aesthetics and the creation of truly beautiful corporations. That is, a world in which corporate activity should constitute "style, beauty, a positive attitude and pleasing experiences" (Dickinson & Svenson, 2000: 3) not only for its members but society as a whole. This holistic vision is summed up well be Sean Blair, Design Director of the UK Design Council (cited in Dickinson & Svenson, 2000: xii) who describes the beautiful corporation as one that will,

...seek people not as human resources, but as human talents, aiming to realize potential not control it. [That] will touch the earth lightly, not using physical resources unnecessarily, but will use resources in new and more efficient ways. The corporation that will dominate tomorrow's business landscape will pursue the social as well as the financial agenda.

The aesthetic at work here then, is perhaps more "post" than "high" modern. This is a vision of contemporary corporations similar to that of Prince Charles' vision for modern architecture; one where design is sensitive to human scale of need, rather than dictated to by abstract principles such as those of "the one best way" or "form follows function".

Nevertheless, there is much here that remains deeply unsettling. What, for example, constitutes this "style" that Dickinson and Svensen constantly refer to both in their subtitle and throughout the work itself? For Schmitt and Simonson (1997: 85) style is the albeit sensitively constructed combination of "color, shape, line and pattern [or] volume, pitch and meter", ultimately quantifiable and certainly marketable. However, for Dickinson and Svensen, style appears to represent a far more metaphysical organizational quality. Style, they acknowledge is in fact an intrinsic quality that cannot simply be invented or acquired—you either have it or you don't. But this does not mean that corporations cannot act in a stylish way, however. For to be stylish is to be attractive, and to be attractive corporations must learn to act with "integrity and honesty", characteristics that the authors view as "prerequisites for success" (Dickinson & Svensen, 2000: 4). Style is also portrayed in terms of corporate "individuality and personality" (Dickinson & Svensen, 2000: 30); it is a way of doing things that can differ between businesses and the contexts within which they operate. So, while the concept of style itself remains esoteric, accessible to those who 'know', illusive for the rest, it also represents the primary ingredient for corporate success.

Yet despite the fact that such apparent mystification may sit well with the ineffable quality of the aesthetic previously disregarded by Schmitt and Simonson, it still appears, however, to serve a very particular function. That being, the placing of the authors and the text itself into a position of power and authority—leaving them relatively free to present their vision of the beautiful corporation free from any need to ground their propositions in anything other than the self-referentiality of their own assertions. Certainly, there is little to convince one that the example of the so-called beautiful corporations they offer up as illustrations of their vision represent anything other than a combination of slick design and the valorization of material aspiration. While the graphic design associated with organizations such as Shell, Mercedes-Benz and UK cable television company OnDigital certainly demonstrate a high degree of corporate aestheticization, there is little evidence to suggest the necessary shift in underlying values and practices that would qualify them, by Dickinson and Svensen's criteria, for the status of a "beautiful corporation". Hence, despite their allusions to something beyond a simple surface aestheticization of organizational activities and presentation, it would seem that Dickinson and Svensen's approach is, on closer inspection not so different from the one taken by Schmitt and Simonson whereby surface aestheticization qualifies as aestheticization per se., and corporate presence exists as the preeminent motivation and goal.

Certainly, when one compares the two approaches, there remains the important common denominator that prevails throughout—their overriding concern with the economic utility of aesthetics for corporate performance within the global marketplace. Design, for example, is championed as the new buzzword for those truly interested in corporate success, replacing now defunct managerial fashions such as TQM and JIT (Dickinson & Svenson, 2000: 41). And, while bottom line and humanistic concerns are combined in the claim that aesthetics can generate both what they term "cultural currency" (Dickinson & Svenson, 2000: 38) and a more humane and productive environment for employees to work in, it is often quite difficult to unravel the distinctions that are made between the pursuit of profit and the professed nurturing of corporate responsibility. Referring, for example, to the thoughts of Jamie Anley, a founder of the design and communication group "JAM", the pursuit of organizational identity through aesthetics is reflected, they suggest, in the belief that it is more admirable for companies to invest in "beautifully designed and made" staff uniforms than it is to spend even more of television advertising (Dickinson & Svenson, 2000: 40). The prioritizing of such activities, while perhaps at first sight a reference to the intrinsic value of providing a more comfortable and stylish working environment for employees, quickly retreats as, on further reading, its impetus derives clearly from the tradition of various 'soft', yet instrumentally focused, employee management strategies associated with other movements and fads such as Human Resource Management (see Legge, 1995) or corporate culturalism (see Parker, 2000).

Furthermore, the opportunities offered by aesthetic management to nurture patterns of normative compliance and ethical attachment by employees is one not lost on those that the authors associate with the popularization of the aesthetics of organizing. Resonating with Featherstone's (1991: 126) comment on contemporary value systems that tend to draw "on tendencies in consumer culture that favour the aestheticization of life, [and] the assumption that the aesthetic life is the ethically good life", the proposition that a clear aesthetic identity can help produce employees that "would have such confidence and satisfaction in the organization that they would, if you met them at a party on a Saturday night, want to press a business card in your hand" (Anley, cited in Dickinson & Svenson, 2000: 41) conflates aesthetic attraction with social value and personal achievement in a way consistent once again with ideas frequently expressed throughout the genre of corporate culturalist "how to" manuals. Furthermore, despite the talk of participation, fluidity and innovative design, the authors requirements that corporate managers learn to "police" the corporate image, to impose "pre-set templates that cannot be changed", undertake the removal "from computer networks all but approved typefaces and introduce publications management systems" (Dickinson & Svenson, 2000: 94) to ensure levels of "standardization and control" in all aesthetic activities, further reinforces the realization that corporate beauty comes at a price. That price, or so it would seem, being the regimentation, standardization and creative closure of the meaning making process as expressed at that very level of organizational practice they so passionately seek to champion.

Aesthetics, Modernity and the Culture Industry

These two particular examples of managerialist literature concerned with the relationship between contemporary organizational life and the aesthetic realm should not, I must stress, be taken as yet to represent anything like a coherent movement within the sphere of contemporary managerial thought. As I have noted, the majority of work that has engaged with the relationship between the aesthetic and the organizational has tended to adopt a far less instrumental orientation, focusing instead on predominantly epistemological or critical issues. Nevertheless, such literature remains significant. For despite the relatively limited level of debate regarding the role of aesthetics management in contemporary work organizations, the practices championed in this literature certainly appear to be increasingly important to the day-to-day operation of a notable range of organizational forms. As I have already suggested this, in large part, can be accounted for by the proliferation of opportunities for organizations to present themselves to the outside world via material that requires constant attention to be paid to its design and presentation. Mission statements, recruitment brochures, web sites, multi-media advertising and the competition that exists around such media all require the closest attention be paid to issues of style, presentation and above all, "feel". It also reflects, however, what I have alluded to as a more general response to our aestheticized culture, one that valorizes above almost all else the qualities of spectacle and display (Urry, 1990). Hence, in what is an increasingly media-saturated environment with its proliferation of sounds and images, organizations involved in the global struggle for market recognition are required to compete in what is an increasingly stimulus rich environment. As such they must seek to pay increasing attention to the aesthetic qualities of everything from its products to its invoice sheets, from its outlets to its office design contribute to the pursuit of that imperative if they are to make an impact on potential stakeholders at each and every opportunity.

Accompanying such a quantitative shift, however, we must, as I also urged earlier, consider the potential qualitative implications of such literature and the developments it both encourages and reflects. In particular, we have to ask just what might it suggest about the nature of contemporary aesthetic experience both within the organizational domain, and the socio-cultural environment more generally. Well, in many respects, it perhaps raises issues similar to those I have explored elsewhere in relation to the question of organizational emotionality (Hancock & Tyler, 2001). This work drew in particular on the ideas of Mestrovic (1997) and his view that we are currently experiencing the dawn of what he terms a *postemotional society*; one in which emotion as an authentically lived experience is being gradually eroded by our constant exposure to mechanized, rationalized and ultimately commodified emotional stimuli. Such postemotionalism is, for Mestrovic (1997: xi) at least, the direct outcome of what he terms the "authenticity industry", consisting largely of a combination of the service and culture industries, and their never ending pursuit of new markets and those mechanisms by which potential consumers may be drawn to them through the generation and then apparent fulfilling of their newly "discovered" emotional needs. Mestrovic's analysis draws together, therefore, a series of apparent developments between the sphere of contemporary work organizations and broader patterns of sociocultural change, in an attempt to establish a fuller picture of the status of emotion in contemporary society.

Now, the similarities between this particular analysis of contemporary emotion and that which is suggested by the material concerned with the management of aesthetics are, I would argue, potentially informative. For whether or not one could convincingly describe the works of the likes of Schmitt and Simonson as part of an authenticity industry per se, certainly their work shares many of the attributes described by Mestrovic, particularly those which he derives from his own analysis of the work of Adorno and Horkheimer (1944/1979, 1991) and their critical account of the "culture industry". Their particular thesis is premised on the view that post-Enlightenment societies can be characterized by the predominance of a mode of rationality that is itself grounded in a drive to domination and control. As such, human activity is considered to be increasingly organized in relation to means, not the consideration of ends, until, as Adorno (1991/2001: 93) notes, "to speak even of culture is to speak of administration whose task is to 'assemble, distribute, evaluate and organize'". This is not to suggest that for Adorno culture and administration are identical in themselves. Rather, he argues that they ideally exist in a state of tension whereby culture serves to celebrate the particular features of life over its generalization, while administration in order to control life, seeks the reverse. Yet the requirements of modern society, and in particular those of capitalism, have unbalanced this tension, increasingly debasing the *lived activity* of culture, and reducing it to a standardized, replicable quantity, which is both easily producible and unquestionably consumable.

While Adorno and Horkheimer's critique of the instrumentalization of culture is perhaps informative in itself in relation to the general incorporation of the "problem of culture" into the field of organizational management, when it comes to the realm of aesthetics it is, I would suggest, particularly pertinent. This is in large part due to the fundamentally emancipatory potential Adorno (1991/2001) ascribed to art in particular, and aesthetic experience in general, due to both its inherent impracticality, and non-conceptual structure; a structure that enables it to articulate the world in a way that is non-reducible to the instrumental categories that contemporary rationality has sought to impose upon it. Yet even in the midst of his attempt to theorize the aesthetic as an enduring realm of critical possibility, he was aware of the ever-encroaching influence of organizational rationality. So while Adorno deliberately opposed culture, as the realm inhabited by art and the aesthetic sensibility, to that of administration and organization he was forced to admit that despite its non-conceptual character, art had not entirely resisted the onslaught of the instrumentalized rationality of modernity.

Today manifestations of extreme artistry can be fostered, produced and presented by official institutions; indeed art is dependent upon such support if it is to be produced at all and find its way to an audience. Yet, at the same time, art denounces everything institutional and official. This gives some evidence of the neutralization of culture and of the irreconcilability with administration of what has been neutralized. Through the sacrifice of its possible relation to praxis, the cultural concept itself becomes an instance of or-

ganization; that which is so provokingly useless in culture is transformed into tolerated negativity or even into something negatively useful—into a lubricant for the system, into something which exists for something else, into untruth*, or into goods of the culture industry calculated for the consumer* (Adorno, 1991/2001: 102 emphasis added).

Like Mestrovic's post-emotional society then, what Adorno appears to lament here is the emergence of a form of post-aestheticism, whereby aesthetic experience is itself little more than the experience of the untruth of the culture industry, albeit one of "beautiful untrue things" (Wilde, 1913: 54). Extrapolating out from this, it could be argued therefore that in creating its systems and frameworks for aesthetic management, in adorning the world in stunning livery, dazzling logos and even, where appropriate, the imagery, sounds and sensations of what may have once been considered the highest of art and culture, the corporate world is equally guilty of reducing aesthetic experience to little more than just another repository of mechanically produced, instrumentally orientated codes and symbols. Having colonized the cognitive and affective realms of both their employees and consumers, it would seem then, that the next assault is to be on the realm of the sensual, albeit in the name of a more beautiful world—naturally.

Critical Considerations

Now, to criticize the aesthetics of the everyday may, in many respects appear to be something of a reactionary activity. After all, if human beings cannot enjoy the mundane sensuality of their surroundings and everyday interactions, what hope is there? Does Featherstone's celebration of the opportunities presented by the commodification of the aesthetic for novel experience, idiosyncratic experimentation and self-expression not deserve to be embraced, rather than dismissed as, at best naive and at worst complicit? Equally, should we not welcome the call for more beautiful corporations from the likes of Dickinson and Svenson, and indeed hope that organizations will embrace the values of design and presentation as their contribution to a more sensually pleasing world? Well, in many respects, this is a well-rehearsed argument, resonating as it does with the schism within cultural studies between the critique of mass culture by the Frankfurt School and its followers and the defenders of what they consider to be the value of the popular (see Fiske, 1989a, 1989b). For the champions of the latter, the resources provided by the culture industry are there to be re-appropriated by the masses – who more often than not succeed in shaping them to their own desires and intentions. However, for the former this remains merely an illusion, determined as it is by the imperatives of mass production and the reductionist logic of cultural commodification. It is, moreover, a debate that appears to show little sign of reaching a satisfactory resolution, with both sides wedded to their respective meta-theoretical and normative positions.

However, the prior existence of such debates should not, I would argue, deter us from continuing to ask those questions which we may feel are of importance to generating a critical understanding of the implications of social change, whatever side of this particular divide they fall on. In this instance that question is, for me at least, what do we take to be the nature of these such aestheticization processes that seem to confront us at both at work and leisure, and what effect, if any, might they have on our capacity for aesthetic experience and judgement? Certainly what such a question does not require, as Adorno and Horkheimer remind us, is a simple finger pointing exercise, seeking out particular individuals for making the world a somehow less authentic place. But perhaps it is a case of following Adorno and Horkheimer's lead, by trying to come to terms with the ways in which "the power of society" as they refer to it (Adorno & Horkheimer, 1944/1979: 124), underwrites a rolling aestheticization of the world. A process by which the ever accelerating demands of a consumer driven market appears to obliterate the need for substance and, in turn, replaces it with the requirement of instant gratification of experience, with the "predominance of the effect, the obvious touch and the technical detail over the work itself" (Adorno and Horkheimer, 1947/1979: 125). For what this suggests is the fundamentally ontological problem of more image and less substance, the experience of an over aestheticization of the world, an explosion of sensuality grounded in large part in the expansion of corporate marketing and organizational aestheticization. Now while this is perhaps something we may initially welcome, for as I suggested above, who would not wish to live in a more aesthetically stimulating world, we should also be sensitive to its potential dangers. Perhaps the most immediate of these being the danger of an over-stimulation of the aesthetic[1]— which in turn numbs our faculty of experience and judgement — a fear echoed by Welsch (1997: 25) recognizing as he does that,

our perception needs not only invigoration and stimulation, but delays, quiet areas and interruptions too... Total aestheticization results in its own opposite. Where everything becomes beautiful, nothing is beautiful any more; continued excitement leads to indifference; aestheticization breaks into anaesthetization.

Thus, once again in a similar vein to Baudrillard's musings over the implications of an over-meditated society on the purposeful nature of the subject (see Hancock, 1999) Welsch counsels us on the dangers of a world made 'too beautiful', one in which the primary danger is the loss of our faculty for aesthetic experience and judgment in the face of an over-aestheticized world. This may not simply be an issue of the potential anesthetization of society however. For it also has important implications for the likes of Adorno's view of the aesthetic as a potentially emancipatory force in contemporary society. For reduced to what appears to be an omnipresent dimension of the everyday in general, and the corporate in particular, the diminution of aesthetic experience can only neutralize its unique mimetic character—its ability to conceive of the world in non-conceptual terms—and in turn witness what is left of it resurrected as little more than a mechanism of conceptual identification, relating stimulus to brand, experience to company or organization. It is not then perhaps a question solely of anesthetization itself, but rather the political implications of an aestheticized environment increasingly driven by the standardized corporate aesthetic; one that embraces our everyday lives telling us its beautiful but untrue things and, in doing so reducing the aesthetic to little more than yet another instrumental carrier of reified 'reality' over utopian possibility.

Conclusion

I mistrust all systematizers and avoid them. The will to a system is a lack of integrity—Nietzsche (1889/1990: 35).

Human history has been characterized by a fundamental struggle between the forces of abstract order and embodied, sensual experience. Yet modernity has witnessed, in large part, the triumph of the former, ushering in an age of reason, of systems and ultimately the dominion of production. So when Wilde observed that for art to have aesthetic value it must tell beautiful untrue things he was, in part, correct. For he recognized that reality, as we experience it, has lost its beauty. Rather, what we have now is a world of order and identity in which what is taken as beauty, or indeed any other facet of authentic aesthetic experience is merely an "appendage of the process of production, without autonomy or substance of its own" (Adorno, 1951/1978: 15). Of course what he forgot was that it does not necessarily mean that what art reveals to us is untrue; merely that it is lacks truth in a world of even greater falsehood. Perhaps it is rather more useful to realize that it is the drive to systematically aestheticize organizational life that is in fact the realm of the beautiful untrue things. For rather than providing the expressive and conceptual space for aesthetic experience to bloom and to flourish in whatever way it might, it in fact intensifies the Enlightenment project of incorporation, seeking to reintegrate the aesthetic into the realm of calculable knowledge and practical utility.

Yet in doing so, it not only debases the aesthetic, depriving it of that which is genuinely identical to it, but also potentially renders it useless in its own cause as well as depriving humanity of its radical potential, its potential to allow us to experience things other than they are. Reduced to yet another tool of the organizational technocrat, the neutralization of the aesthetic risks becoming absolute, until it becomes indistinguishable in a world where aesthetic experience is reduced to nothing more than the deadened apprehension of the sterile landscape of society, and judgment an association of a contrived meaning with an appropriate corporate livery.

References

Adorno, T. (1978). *Minima moralia: Reflections from damaged life* (E.F.N Jephcott, Trans.) London: Verso. (Original work published 1951)

Adorno, T. (2001). *The culture industry: Selected essays on mass culture* (J. Bernstein, Ed.). London: Routledge. (Original work published 1991)

Adorno, T., & Horkheimer, M. (1979). *Dialectic of enlightenment.* (J. Cumming, Trans.). London: Verso. (Original work published 1944)

Baudrillard, J. (1981). For *a critique of the political economy of the sign* (C. Levin, Trans.). St Louis, MO: Telos. (Original work published 1972)

Berg, P., & Kreiner, K. (1990). Corporate architecture: turning physical settings into symbolic resources. In P. Gagliardi (Ed.), *Symbols and artifacts: Views of the corporate landscape* (pp. 41-68). Berlin: de Gruyter.

Carr, A. (2002, July). *The modernist pre-occupation with speed: A psychoanalytic and critical reading.* Paper presented at The 20th Anniversary Standing Conference on Organizational Symbolism, Budapest, Hungary.

Carter, P., & Jackson, N. (2000). An-aestehtics. In S. Linstead & H. Höpfl (Eds.), *Aesthetics and organization* (pp. 180-196). London: Sage.

Cooper, R., & Sawaf, A. (1998). *Executive EQ.* New York: Orion.

Deal, T., & Kennedy, A. (1982). *Corporate culture: The rites and rituals of corporate life.* Reading, Mass: Addison-Wesley.

Dickinson, P., & Svensen, N. (2000). *Beautiful corporations: corporate style in action.* Harlow: Pearson Education.

Featherstone, M. (1991). *Consumer culture and postmodernism.* London: Sage

Fiske, J. (1989a). *Understanding popular culture.* London: Routledge

Fiske, J. (1989b). *Reading the popular.* London: Routledge.

Gagliardi, P. (1990). Artifacts as pathways and remains of organizational life. In P. Gagliardi (Ed.), *Symbols and artifacts: views of the corporate landscape* (pp. 3-38). Berlin: de Gruyter.

Gagliardi, P. (1996). Exploring the aesthetic side of organizational life. In S. Clegg, C. Hardy and W. Nord (Eds.), *Handbook of organization studies* (pp. 565-580). London: Sage.

Gardner, D. (2001, August). Sprinting out of the blocks in the world of aesthetics, *The Herald*, 22.

Habermas, J. (1984). *The theory of communicative action volume one: Reason and the rationalization of society.* Cambridge: Polity. (Original work published 1981)

Hancock, P. (1999). Baudrillard and the metaphysics of motivation: A reappraisal of corporate culturalism in the light of the work and ideas of Jean Baudrillard, *Journal of Management Studies*, 36, 155-75.

Hancock, P., & Tyler, M. (2000). "The look of love": Gender and the organization of aesthetics. In J. Hassard, R. Holliday & H. Willmott (Eds.), *Body and organization* (pp. 108-129). London: Sage.

Hancock, P., & Tyler, M. (2001). *Work, postmodernism and organization: a critical introduction.* London: Sage.

Höpfl, H. (2000). The aesthetics of reticence: Collections and recollections. In S. Linstead & H. Höpfl (Eds.), *The aesthetics of organization* (pp. 93-110). London: Sage.

Jacobson, M. (1993). *Art and business.* London: Thames and Hudson.

Jacobson, M. (1996). Art and business in a brave new world.

Organization, 3, 243-248.

Kant, I. (1952). *The critique of judgement* (J. Creed, Trans.). Oxford: Clarendon Press. (Original work published 1790)

Klein, N. (2001). *No logo*. London: Flamingo. (Original work published 1999)

Larsen, J. & Schultz, M. (1990). Artifacts in a bureaucratic monastery. In P. Gagliardi (Ed.), *Symbols and artifacts: Views of the corporate landscape* (pp. 281 – 302). Berlin: de Gruyter.

Legge, K. (1995). *Human resource management: Rhetorics and realities*. Basingstoke: Macmillan Business.

Marcuse, H. (1979). *The aesthetic dimension: Toward a critique of Marxist aesthetics*. London: Macmillan. (Original work published 1978)

Meares, R. (1992). *The metaphor of play*. Melbourne, Australia: Hill of Content.

Meares, R., & Coombes, T. (1994). A drive to play: Evolution and psychotherapeutic theory. *Australian and New Zealand Journal of Psychiatry, 28*, 58-67.

Mestrovic, S. (1997). *Postemotional society*. London: Sage.

Nietzsche, F. (1990). *Twilight of the idols*. London: Penguin. (Original work published 1889)

Olins, W. (1989). *Corporate identity: making business strategy visible through design*. London: Thames and Hudson.

Parker, M. (2000). *Organizational culture and identity*. London: Sage.

Plato, (1987). *The Republic* (D. Lee, Trans.) (2nd ed.). London: Penguin. (This translation published 1955)

Pollock, L. (2000). That's infotainment. *People Management, 25*(6), 19-23.

Schmitt, B. (2000). *Experiential marketing: How to get customers to sense, feel, think, act, relate to your company and brands*. New York, NY: Free Press.

Schmitt, B., Simonson, A., & Marcus, J. (1995). Managing corporate, image and identity. *Long Range Planning, 28*(5), 82-92.

Schmitt, B. & Simonson, A. (1997). *Marketing aesthetics: The strategic management of brands, identity and image*. New York, NY: Free Press.

Strati, A. (1990). Aesthetics and organizational skill. In B.A. Turner, (Ed.), *Organizational symbolism* (pp. 207-22). Berlin: De Gruyter.

Strati, A. (1992). Aesthetic understanding of organizational life.

Academy of Management Review, 17, 568-81.
Strati, A. (1996). Organizations viewed through the lens of aesthetics. *Organization, 3*, 209-218.
Strati, A. (1999). *Organization and aesthetics.* London: Sage.
Strati, A. (2000a). The aesthetic approach in organization studies. In S. Linstead, H. & Höpfl (Eds.), *The aesthetics of organization* (pp. 13-34). London: Sage.
Strati, A. (2000b). *Theory and method in organization studies.* London: Sage.
Thompson, P., Warhurst, C., & Callaghan, G. (2000). Human capital or capitalising on humanity? Knowledge, skills and competencies in interactive service work. In C. Prichard, R. Hull, M. Chumer & H. Willmott (Eds.), *Managing knowledge: critical investigations of work and learning* (pp. 122-140). Basingstoke: Macmillan.
Urry, J. (1990). *The tourist gaze: Leisure and travel in contemporary societies.* London: Sage.
Welsch, W. (1997). *Undoing aesthetics.* London: Sage.
Wilde, O. (1913). *The decay of lying.* In *Intentions* (pp. 1-54). London: Methuen & Co. (Original work published 1905)
Witkin, R. (1990). The aesthetic imperative of rational-technical machinery: A study in organizational control through the design of artefacts. In P. Gagliardi (Ed.), *Symbols and artifacts: Views of the corporate landscape* (pp. 325-338). Berlin: de Gruyter.

Notes

[1] Adrian Carr (2002) and Russell Meares (1992) have warned that, at a more general level, there are psychological consequences of an environment that is over-stimulating. A phenomenon dubbed "stimulus entrapment" may ensue. Stimulus entrapment is a notion that through continual hypervigilance externally, a person fails to develop an "inner self voice" and, as a result, experiences feelings of "emptiness". A lack of an ability to self reflect, makes these individuals prone to external locus of control and/or to a false self that is often one dimensional. "They live as if at the mercy of the environment, in a hypertrophy of the 'real' " (Meares & Coombes, 1994: 66). Further, Carr (2002) argues that the increasing pace of our capitalist society, that demands the instantaneous, has itself demanded and sustained a state of external hypervigilance, maintaining a need for societal personas while simultaneously mitigating against individuality.

www.ingramcontent.com/pod-product-compliance
Lightning Source LLC
La Vergne TN
LVHW050630100826
845148LV00011B/1805

* 9 7 8 0 9 8 1 7 0 3 2 5 1 *